T0148749

FLYING BLIND

ADVANCE PRAISE FOR THE BOOK

'Tracing the story of India's foreign policy, from the earliest post-Independence years to the present day, Mohamed Zeeshan writes fluently on one of the great existential questions for any nation: What is our place in the world? With meticulous detail and a wary eye on East and West, Zeeshan explains our foreign-policy history while making a passionate case for a more globally involved India, working to better the complex world it finds itself in. I applaud this young scholar and look forward to the evolution of his future work.'—Shashi Tharoor, MP

'A youthful and starkly unalloyed perspective of India's foreign policy. Mohamed Zeeshan's fresh examination of Indian diplomacy's "hardy perennials" makes for a refreshing read.'—Syed Akbaruddin, former Indian ambassador to the United Nations

'International relations are highly volatile these days, and it is essential for nation-states to craft strategies that enable them to navigate successfully a world order in great flux. This is especially true for emerging powers like India. This timely and important new book, by one of India's most impressive young thought leaders, lays out a much-needed foreign policy vision for New Delhi.'—Michael Kugelman, noted South Asia commentator and deputy director of the Asia Program, Wilson Center, Washington DC

'India's foreign policy is at a major crossroads, caught between domestic political temptations and external constraints, faced with the everydayness of an increasingly rebellious and hostile neighbourhood, and having to make far-reaching strategic choices, something the country is not used to. The age of fence-sitting may be over, as also the heart-warming stories of India's geopolitical rise. Mohamed Zeeshan's highly accessible and smartly written book captures the dilemmas of making strategic decisions that will shape India's foreign policy for a long time to come.'—Happymon Jacob, professor, Jawaharlal Nehru University, and columnist, *The Hindu*

'In most parts of the world, it is commonly understood that all politics are locally determined. But in the twenty-first century, globalizing, interdependent world, it is crucial for all citizens of nation-states to recognize the importance of their country's interactions with other countries. Mohamed Zeeshan eloquently and passionately makes the case for understanding foreign policy in the context of India's economic aspirations.'—Vishakha N. Desai, senior adviser for global affairs to the president and chair, Committee on Global Thought, Columbia University

FLYING BLIND

INDIA'S QUEST FOR GLOBAL LEADERSHIP

Mohamed Zeeshan

VINTAGE
An imprint of Penguin Random House

VINTAGE

USA | Canada | UK | Ireland | Australia
New Zealand | India | South Africa | China

Vintage is part of the Penguin Random House group of companies
whose addresses can be found at global.penguinrandomhouse.com

Published by Penguin Random House India Pvt. Ltd
7th Floor, Infinity Tower C, DLF Cyber City,
Gurgaon 122 002, Haryana, India

First published in Vintage by Penguin Random House India 2021

Copyright © Mohamed Zeeshan 2021

All rights reserved

10 9 8 7 6 5 4 3 2 1

ISBN 9780670094462

Typeset in Bembo Std by Manipal Technologies Limited, Manipal
Printed at Replika Press Pvt. Ltd, India

www.penguin.co.in

To my late grandmother, Khyrunneisa Khader, whose unconditional support and unfailing belief in me I will forever cherish and forever miss

Contents

Preface

When I explain to Indian friends that India should start playing a more proactive role in international affairs, they often stop me midway and ask, 'Why?' That is a reasonable question. There will always be a compelling moral case for the world's largest democracy to help people in faraway lands. But India is still a developing country with several problems back home. Its resources are limited, and should be better spent on domestic problems, rather than on foreign troubles.

Given the complexities of India's vast and diverse domestic landscape, few Indians spend much time worrying about problems in other parts of the world. When the Indian media covers foreign events, it does so in a rather cursory manner. Foreign policy analysis is almost entirely consumed by the immediate neighbourhood— and generally, just Pakistan. To Indians who reside abroad, this insularity is amply obvious. Just compare a day's news coverage in the *New York Times* to the same day's news in any leading Indian English daily. While the *Times* typically devotes five or six pages to non-US news each day, English dailies in India print a meagre page and a half, at most, of international news.

As India grows in size and significance, this insularity can have costs, both at home and abroad. In the absence of credible ground reporting in foreign countries, the public is forced to speculate wildly about the rest of the world. At its worst, this means dangerous and provocative sensationalism in national discourse, even hate-filled public rhetoric: Many Indians often paint neighbours as existential threats, and leaders have been guilty of chest-thumping at the expense of important allies.

Insularity also means that Indians rarely hold their governments accountable for foreign policy. Let's face it, foreign policy doesn't win you votes. No Indian prime minister has ever won office because of his or her foreign policy acumen, and most political frontrunners in India have had little or no experience with diplomacy or international affairs. When I asked one Indian diplomat what she reckons is the difference between the Indian Foreign Service (IFS) and its more celebrated cousin, the Indian Administrative Service, she simply said, 'We don't get bothered by politicians.'

But this is a problem. Few Indians realize the extent to which they overestimate India's global influence, or the money spent by the government on essential foreign relations. In 2018, the Pew Global Attitudes survey asked respondents whether India was more important, as important or less important in the world as compared to ten years ago. In only one country did more than 50 per cent of the people say that India was now more important: That country was India. In the other twenty-six countries polled, more than a third said India was no more important in 2018 than in 2008. A further 22 per cent said that India had in fact become *less important* in world affairs in those ten years. There was something even worse about the results of this poll: The most sceptical about India's importance were *developing countries*—Brazil, Mexico, Argentina, South Africa, the Philippines, Indonesia and the like.[1]

For a country that routinely talks of itself as a leader of the developing world, these figures should be disturbing. Yet, India spends scant resources on this perception problem—or on developing its global influence. To start with, the IFS is woefully understaffed. By some estimates, India has about as many diplomats serving its needs as Singapore—a city-state with just over a quarter of the population of Delhi. India's counterparts in the emerging world fare much better: Brazil, for instance, has over *twice* as many serving diplomats (with a population roughly the same as the state of Uttar Pradesh). Sometimes, therefore, a single officer must work on such disparate issues as trade and military policy from a single desk, often left with little space to pay sufficient attention to either.

But the question still stands: Why should Indians care about foreign policy? The answer is simple: Indians *need* their government to be more powerful and influential around the world, in order to be able to fulfil the needs of ordinary Indians both at home and abroad.

At no point in history has the average Indian been as thoroughly globalized as today. Each day, she wakes up to an alarm clock made in China, eats breakfast cereal invented in America, uses a watch designed by the Japanese, and drives a car engineered in Germany, fuelled by oil from the Middle East. In 1960, India's exports and imports together amounted to less than a tenth of the GDP. By 2014, they weighed up more than four-tenths. In 2016, there were 3,60,000 Indian students in universities overseas, and the year before, almost 16 million Indians were resident abroad—the most for any country that year, according to United Nations data.

The purpose of foreign policy is to create favourable conditions for all of these Indian students, businesses and workers abroad. Indians aspiring to gain international exposure and experience should feel the security of a strong Indian passport and an influential Indian government. Back home, India's farmers and engineers need favourable trade conditions to flourish and prosper. Fishermen need rights over marine resources to sustain their livelihoods. Labourers toiling in the Gulf to send money for families back home need better working and living conditions. Just as importantly, India needs global support against threats to its own security, whether from terrorists or from sovereign states.

Yet, while India has grown over the years, it is still far from fulfilling all these expectations. India still struggles to find allies and global support in the aftermath of cross-border terror attacks, which have continued unabated in recent years. Over the last two Indian governments, sudden changes to immigration laws in countries such as Malaysia and Kuwait left the futures of Indian workers and families hanging in the balance. Reports have brought to light the inhuman working conditions of some Indian labourers in parts of the Gulf; as the novel coronavirus (COVID-19) spread through the world, Indian migrant workers found themselves trapped in overcrowded labour camps with no support from their host governments.

Meanwhile, fugitives of Indian law have escaped the country and successfully taken refuge abroad, while India has looked on helplessly. And India's arms-length approach to conflicts in Africa and the Middle East has meant that New Delhi has had little or no say on the course of events in those places, while several Indian civilians have been caught in the crossfire. During Yemen's civil war, for instance, India had to evacuate thousands of its citizens after the death toll kept mounting in 2015.

Perhaps the most telling grassroots evidence of India's weak foreign influence is, quite simply, the power of the Indian passport itself. Each year, the International Air Transport Association (IATA) and a global consultancy firm, Henley & Partners, release a Henley Passport Index that ranks countries according to the travel freedom that their citizens enjoy.* India has been shockingly poor on the index

---

* The Index defined 'travel freedom' as the right of citizens to enter a foreign country without visa restrictions. A country also gained points on the index if its citizens enjoyed the benefits of visas on arrival or e-visas in other countries.

every year. As of November 2020, it ranked a lowly 82nd out of 106 positions, tied with Tajikistan—and far below Brazil, Mexico, China or even Zimbabwe. In all, while India issues visas on arrival or e-visas to over 100 countries (including for business purposes), Indian citizens enjoy similar privileges only in fifty-eight countries.

The weakness of the Indian passport is—ironically—also a key cause of 'brain drain': the permanent loss of Indian skill and talent to other countries. With immigration restrictions the way they are, only the smartest and brightest of Indians often manage to migrate overseas to high-paying jobs or alluring opportunities. And they often change their citizenship once they are out, owing to the weakness of the Indian passport. While working in the Middle East, I often heard very telling first-hand accounts from highly skilled, well-educated Indian professionals who first migrated to Australia or Canada, changed their passport, and then moved to the Middle East for posh, high-paying jobs on their new passport. At many local firms in the Middle East, citizens from Western countries are in fact even *paid more* for the same kind of work. For all these reasons, Henley & Partners—the firm which publishes the Passport Index each year—even has a 'citizenship by investment' programme, which helps the wealthy acquire an alternative passport for higher travel freedom.

The weakness of a country's passport, or its inability to prevail in trade negotiations, is a direct consequence of weak global influence. Yet, for decades, India's global influence has never quite featured in discussions on the objectives of Indian foreign policy. Indian foreign policy has traditionally been restricted to the analysis of bilateral transactions—trade agreements, defence equipment purchases, infrastructure deals and the like. By contrast, limited time and strategic thinking is spent on the development of a coherent strategic vision that would increase India's global power and influence. State visits by prime ministers have often seemed more like the peripatetic travels of a CEO, revolving around

MoUs and business deals rather than political influence or strategic cooperation.

This practice of foreign policy was designed for a much weaker India, which was endowed with limited resources and aspirations, a far less globalized economy, and several existential threats to the country's survival. Today, India has the world's second largest military, third largest defence budget, and fifth largest economy. Its growing global engagement needs an attitude of expanding national power and influence, rather than foreign relations for mere material survival. This book is an effort to explore what this reorientation in India's foreign policy should look like.

Introduction

The Pursuit of Influence

Are the Rich Always Influential?

Few medieval kingdoms were made of the sort of ostentatious wealth that defined the Mughal state. Merchants and ambassadors flocked to the Mughal court all through the medieval ages, hoping to take part in the prosperity. Among those seeking to court the Mughals in the early 1600s was the king of England. In 1615, King James sent his distinguished envoy Sir Thomas Roe, bearing a letter for the Mughal emperor.

James was not making any outlandish demands of the wealthy Mughal emperor; there was no talk of 'colonialism', 'domination' or British influence over India. In fact, James was merely asking the Mughals for 'amity' and rights for the English East India Company

to trade in India. Yet, no less than four merchant-ambassadors
had sailed to India before Roe, hoping to receive a response from
Jahangir. All four had failed spectacularly.

In 1609, William Hawkins became James's first envoy in
Agra, seeking to persuade Jahangir with the king's letter. But the
attempt was botched just days into the effort. Hawkins was expelled
unceremoniously by Jahangir, after he entered the Mughal court in
an inebriated state. Soon, Hawkins was followed from London by
Paul Canning, whose fate turned out much worse. After a long and
tiring journey to India, Canning was duly deflected away into the
hands of the Mughal governor of customs, while his accompanying
cornet player was taken to Jahangir for the entertainment of his court.

London then sent Thomas Kerridge to try a third time. But by
now, the Mughal emperor was increasingly dismayed. On his first
day in Agra, Kerridge was kept waiting without admission into the
Mughal court. The next day, Jahangir asked for his lavish turban as a
gift, before turning him away once more to the governor of customs.

Yet, arguably the most humiliating Mughal reception was
reserved for Kerridge's successor—and London's fourth attempt at
courting the Mughals—William Edwards. Hoping to impress the
Mughal emperor with his ill-advised bravado, Edwards was kicked
and spurned by the emperor's porters at the court gates, with little
regard for title or representation.[1]

When Roe landed in India as a last-gasp fifth attempt, all this
made him understandably anxious. Travelling inland through India
in late 1615, Roe complained in writing to the English East India
Company about the quality of the presents he was carrying to the
Mughal court: 'I am worst furnished, having nothing at all,' he
lamented. 'Here are nothing esteemed but of the best sorts: good
cloth and fine, and rich pictures . . . so they laugh at us for such as
we bring.'

The Mughals were extremely wealthy. For most of history,
India accounted for about a third or more of the world's total

economic output, all the way up until the Industrial Revolution in the late eighteenth century. By the 1600s, Mughal India had accumulated so much wealth that there was little for the emperor to do, apart from erecting richly decorated palaces and monuments—such as, indeed, the Taj Mahal itself. In common thinking, all that wealth should have made India, under the Mughals, an extremely influential global superpower. Wealth, after all, often conjures up images of influence and domination.

Yet, while wealth *could* have led to global influence, at no point would one say that the Mughals wielded 'global influence'; no Mughal emperor ever shaped the course of events in Europe, Africa or even other parts of Asia. In fact, even at their zenith, the Mughals struggled to assert political influence over parts of the Indian peninsula itself.*

But what then is 'influence'? 'Influence' is the ability to shape events, gain bargaining power for negotiations, and—at its crassest—would also include the power to use incentives in order to shape the behaviour of others. 'Influential powers' are states that are important to the well-being and security of other countries, which means countries have a stake in their welfare. Regional and global powers can be thought to have 'influence' if they are able to mobilize states to act in a certain manner, against a common threat or in pursuit of a common purpose.

This ability to mobilize different states towards a common purpose can be gained and exercised in various ways—wealth being only one of them. In the modern era, Japan is far wealthier than Russia, by most economic measures. The

---

* 'Political influence' is different from 'sovereignty'. Sovereignty is the right to rule over a certain territory as its only master; political influence is the ability to shape political events. There were some Mughal emperors, in fact, who struggled to maintain political influence even over areas where they were 'sovereign'. This distinction is key: political influence is not necessarily about conquest and war.

Japanese economy is worth over four times Russia's, with fewer people than in Russia. Japan is also the fourth largest exporter and fifth largest importer in the world; Russia ranks 13th and 22nd. Yet, on most international issues, Russia holds the aces, not Japan. When countries want to prevent Iran from getting a nuclear weapon, they call for cooperation from Russia, not Japan. When the civil war in Syria is raging, Russia calls the shots, not Japan. While on economic issues Japan is arguably far more influential than Russia, on all political and security matters which dominate the foreign policy of most countries, Moscow is far more significant.

The answer to why Russia wields influence that far outsizes its economic heft is complicated: Moscow has a far more developed military arsenal, equipped with nuclear weapons; it holds a veto in the UN Security Council; it exports weapons to regimes and militias around the world. But perhaps most importantly, Moscow has deployed its national power around the world and has a coherent strategic vision with well-defined foreign policy objectives. It knows what it wants and it is willing to get it. It makes logically consistent decisions on whom to support and whom to oppose in conflicts around the world, and uses its allies effectively in pursuing those common goals.

India is in many ways as economically influential as Japan. It now has a larger economy on purchasing power parity (PPP) terms than Japan, a young and upcoming middle-class population, one of the fastest-growing consumer markets in the world, and more promising demographics than Japan. Most investors think of the future of the global economy as being in India, not in Japan. If India doesn't already have economic influence, it is pre-ordained to, because of the sheer size of numbers. Regardless of poor infrastructure and corruption, any number multiplied by a billion is a very large number and therefore consequential for economic well-being everywhere else.

But what India needs to build is political presence and influence around the world. The foreign policies of most states around the world are dominated by political interests rather than economic interests. The old adage in the most significant discussions at the United Nations these days is 'politics first', for without political stability, there cannot be an economy. India needs to build a narrative that would contribute towards the political stability and well-being of countries around the world—and it needs to be credible, coherent and reliable in its pursuit of that agenda. If India begins to represent the needs of people in other countries, and does so in a consistent and reliable manner, it will gain influence by benefiting them.*

Think of why one's elected representative is important. It isn't merely law-making powers that make a parliamentarian influential. A parliamentarian is influential because his constituency believes that he will act in ways that will fulfil *their* needs and interests. That logic of democracy works quite the same way on the global stage. And as with every political leader, a rising global power must also campaign for influence on the back of a coherent narrative and story.

Yet, this isn't to argue that India should act against its *own* interests. In building its foreign policy narrative, India ought to actively seek common ground between its own needs and abilities, and those of allies around the world. If India pursues policies that are inconsistent with its own needs or its own identity—simply to appease other countries or allies—those policies will not last, and they certainly won't be credible in the eyes of the benefactor.

---

* Let me add: in the case of stable states with advanced economies (think Japan or South Korea), economic interests are more important, and by the same logic as here, if India represents those economic interests, it will gain political influence in these countries by being important to them. However, the vast majority of today's countries are *not* Japan or South Korea and for many, political interests still trump economic interests.

All of this means that New Delhi needs to do things that it hasn't had to do in decades: define an identity for India on the global stage and take a stand on issues that matter to people in distant parts of the world. That starts with the definition of what India is, what India wants, and what India can do.

Knowledge of Self Is Wisdom

To many outside observers, there isn't one 'India' but many 'Indias'. In 1931, at the height of India's freedom movement, Winston Churchill scoffed at the idea that India could become an independent nation-state. 'India is no more a political personality than Europe,' he told the Constitutional Club in London. 'India is a geographical term . . . [and] no more a united nation than the Equator.'

Churchill was wrong about India in several ways, but on this particular description, most people would agree. Some eighty years later, while recalling his tours across the country, Australian cricket legend Matthew Hayden wrote, '[There is] no such thing as a stereotypical Indian. India changes for every hundred kilometres.'[2] I have often reflected on this myself. India is one of the few countries in the world where one can hop on a train in one state, surrounded by one culture, one language and one style of attire, and get off a few hundred kilometres away, only to see an entirely different culture, an altogether different language and an unrecognizably different dressing style.

Over the years, the dizzying diversity in culture and society was accompanied by varied political practices and records of governance across the country. Some of the disparity across India would seem simply unreasonable. In 2017–18, India's richest state, Goa, had a real per capita GDP over *twelve times* that of India's poorest state: Bihar. The most startling image of this large disparity in income, aspiration and needs is the Mumbai skyline itself—Asia's largest slum is located just minutes away from the world's costliest residence, belonging to billionaire Mukesh Ambani.

This diversity in needs, interests and aspirations across India is a more significant foreign policy challenge than most people would recognize. In defining the needs and interests for all of India— and, in turn, a global agenda that would represent the wildly different aspirations of each Indian—foreign policy strategists face a tricky balancing act. If there are many 'Indias'—each with different necessities and different aspirations—and each one must be represented, what does *all* of India stand for on the global stage?

When India became independent in 1947, it *did* in fact have a coherent narrative on the world stage. At the time, Prime Minister Jawaharlal Nehru dug into the deep reservoirs of principled idealism that had inspired India's noble struggle for freedom. Indian diplomats frequently spoke on the world stage on such things as colonialism, racism, foreign exploitation, non-violent dispute settlement, and mutual respect for sovereignty. In partnership with China, Nehru pioneered what came to be known as the Panchsheel, or the 'five principles of peaceful coexistence'—in some sense, an Eastern version of the Atlantic Charter. From there, Nehru formed the Non-Aligned Movement (NAM), with the intent of keeping newly sovereign states out of the traps and mines of the Cold War.

Nehru read the needs of the postcolonial world right, and essentially offered just what India's peers in Asia, Africa and Latin America were looking for. Starting from the 1950s, multiple African states declared independence from Europe. Each was looking for a global spokesperson to represent its outrage against racism, colonialism and imperial exploitation on the international stage. These ideals, after all, formed the crux of freedom movements across Asia and Africa, and were necessary for uniting disparate tribes and factions into one complicated Tanzania or Ghana.

Nehru delivered the narrative, and it worked. As newly independent African states were populating the United Nations through the 1960s, India became the spokesperson for half the world, far outsizing its crippling material limitations. While New Delhi asked Washington and Moscow for food aid, it was also influential in the mediation of crises in Korea and Indochina. The trump card was that India acted as a credible neutral voice with the support of the postcolonial world. When civil war broke out in the Congo, the then UN secretary general, Dag Hammarskjöld, appointed a senior Indian diplomat, Rajeshwar Dayal, as his special representative, and told him, 'The role of Nehru will now be decisive.'[3] Hammarskjöld was right. India went on to lead the UN peacekeeping mission in the Congo, and its influence kept the UN aligned in favour of the Congolese government, despite Western interests pulling in the opposite direction.

But while its postcolonial victim's narrative had won support and influence in several states across the world, India found that it had far overshot its material capabilities. The 1960s were a tumultuous decade. Two years in, China exposed India's military frailties in an extended battle along the Himalayas. After days of fighting between the two countries, India had lost nearly 1400 of its soldiers, and a further 1700 were missing. Almost 4000 Indian men had been captured by the Chinese, of whom twenty-six died in captivity. Yet, not a single Chinese soldier could be captured in return.[4] Shortly afterwards, 30 million people in Bihar faced scarcity of food and water, triggering a nationwide scare of famine. Until the Green Revolution that began a few years later, India was heavily dependent on food aid from—ironically—the United States.

Yet, it was the decisive military defeat against China which proved to be a turning point in Indian foreign policy. Despite the influence that New Delhi wielded across Africa and postcolonial Asia, the limits of its national power had been horrifyingly exposed by Beijing. Even India's postcolonial allies could not be of any support during the war. The lesson was that, in building its global narrative, India had acted in ways that turned out to be inconsistent with its own needs and interests. While India battled China in the Himalayas, some Indian troops were still occupied in the Congo. It was a crisis of self-awareness, which in many ways continues to this day.

Give the People What They Want

In the spring of 2015, President Goodluck Jonathan of Nigeria handed over power to Muhammadu Buhari after Buhari won a tense presidential election. As we watched the news together, a puzzled Nigerian friend asked me, 'How do you get prime ministers in your country to vacate office after losing an election?'

The question had context. That year, Buhari was becoming the first president in Nigerian history to win power through a democratic election. Since 1999, Jonathan's party, the People's Democratic Party, had ruled virtually unopposed with few questions asked. Buhari himself had managed an earlier stint as president in 1983 only after a military coup. That had followed an earlier coup in 1975 by Nigeria's fifth president, Olusegun Obasanjo, who had himself succeeded a military general as head of state.

Yet, Nigeria is arguably one of the success stories of Africa. Since achieving independence in the 1960s, Africa has seen some 200 coups or attempted coups in nearly every country in the north, west and east. If you wanted to become head of state, you had one of two options: pull together an armed rebel militia to storm the capital, or head the military and beat the rebels to the race. Once in power, the president almost invariably secured himself by replacing all senior military personnel and government servants with his own loyalists. But the loyalists often came from his own clan or native region, thereby marginalizing other communities in national politics and sowing the seeds of yet another civil war. In recent years, the chaos and vacuum in some parts of the continent has been filled by global terrorist groups—Boko Haram in Nigeria, Al Shabaab in Somalia, and Al Qaeda in Mali.

In result, after nearly six decades since the end of colonialism in Africa, some two-thirds of the security conflicts reviewed by the UN Security Council today are in Africa. The bulk of UN peacekeeping—and most Indian troops stationed under the UN flag—is also in Africa.

But this isn't just the story of Africa. Perhaps the biggest crisis in international politics today is the ubiquity of fragile and weak states across the postcolonial world—most of which are characterized by struggles over the definition of national identity, threats to basic human rights, and weak and dysfunctional political and economic institutions that often become the cause of instability, poverty and terrorism. Think of Myanmar, which is still struggling to reconcile its national identity with the presence of the stateless Rohingyas, while at the same time seeking to build nascent democratic institutions after decades of despotic military rule. Or think of Mexico and Colombia, where the spectre of drug cartels comes in the way of building fair and functional governance institutions that can inspire confidence among the people. In Venezuela and Egypt, the press is still heavily censored, freedoms are routinely suppressed, and development consequently impeded. All these countries are perennially at risk of periodic street protests against the ruling establishment.

In the decades that followed India's independence, several countries became free around the world, giving Nehru the opportunity to become a spokesperson for the interests of the postcolonial world. But people in the postcolonial world are no longer quite as interested in talk of racism, colonialism and exploitation by the French or the British; they are more interested in building a peaceful and stable nation, with functional state institutions that guarantee long-term stability and development. Even in countries where politics is fairly stable and functional, popular opinion has been pushing for the improvement of governance institutions, in order to increase transparency, accountability and economic development. The impetus behind the Sustainable Development Goals at the UN—which call for action on precisely these and other related issues—came from the *developing world*, from countries such as Guatemala and Mexico, and not from London or Washington.

In the aftermath of the COVID-19 pandemic, the clamour for development institutions around the world will only get louder. Countries suffering from weak governance capacity and—worse—civil war and violence are a natural threat to global health, development and security. Global cooperation will necessarily need to address these gaps in public systems worldwide.

What does all this mean for New Delhi? For years now, India has stood out in the postcolonial world as one among very few stable democratic states, with an economy that has long been on the move. If Indian strategists are wondering what role New Delhi should play on the world stage, they should look no further than India's own long-standing and globally recognized strengths. As one might say about domestic politics, just so even in international politics: give the people what they want.

No Man's Land

The war against China in 1962 was arguably the most influential turning point in independent India's foreign policy. It drove home to Indians the importance of national security and of the need for material development and military prowess. Most significantly, it somewhat hurt the credibility of Nehruvian idealism in Indian strategic circles. In the years that followed, Nehru's daughter, Indira Gandhi, took a decidedly more hawkish approach to the neighbourhood and the world. India conducted its first nuclear test in the 1970s, while the Green Revolution ran in parallel to boost food security and self-reliance. The Indian military regained some of its morale through its success in the liberation of Bangladesh in 1971.

Two decades later, economic liberalization brought a windfall after a crushing currency crisis. In the twenty-five years from 1991 to 2016, India's per capita income more than tripled from around $530 to over $1800 (in constant terms at 2010 prices). It had remained largely stagnant for several years prior.

All this nation-building took place under a largely hawkish foreign policy. Since India's war with China in 1962, New Delhi has chased what it calls 'strategic independence'—a go-it-yourself foreign policy, free of alliance obligations and ideology, and coloured by a deep scepticism of international politics. But this was a foreign policy largely focused on the neighbourhood, rather than outside. For the most part, India took a hiatus from the world stage during its phase of nation-building. And its attitude towards its neighbours was one of defence rather than cooperation—all that it wanted in South Asia was to keep potential external threats from entering: terrorists from Pakistan, fake currency from Nepal, and migrants from Bangladesh.

This neighbourhood-centric hawkish foreign policy is the one that most Indians would recognize at home. In New York, however, India's narrative at the UN has sometimes been at odds with this rather cynical outlook. There, India continues to be avowedly Nehruvian and globalist—pushing resolutions aimed at anti-colonialism, anti-racism, and solidarity with the postcolonial oppressed. On matters of global economic governance, it's more of the same—New Delhi often speaks of the exploitation of postcolonial developing states by unfair trade practices and the like.

On occasions, India has juggled Mrs Gandhi's hawkish scepticism with Nehru's globalist idealism while dealing with the same singular issue, thereby putting India's foreign policy in no man's land. When democracy was suppressed in the Maldives and

Myanmar, New Delhi was unsure whether to approach the junta regimes with Nehruvian idealism—calling for strengthening of democracy—or whether to put ideology in cold storage and think more as Mrs Gandhi might have done. Similarly, refugee crises in South East Asia were met with the same ambivalence and—worse—ambiguity from strategic thinkers and policymakers in New Delhi.

The story of dilemmas in Indian foreign policy has become an increasingly obvious tradition in recent years. India seems rather unsure over whether it should recognize its identity as a democratic power on the world stage or whether it should stand for the ideals of its early foreign policy under Nehru. Perhaps most importantly, Indians don't often talk about what India's national interests *really are*.

Most books on Indian foreign policy tend to focus more on the specifics of bilateral relationships, rather than on a coherent global strategic agenda. But this book will not contain any analysis on individual treaties or initiatives; there are already many excellent books on them. You will not, for instance, find an inquiry in this book into recent deals between the US and India on defence technology. Instead, I will explore the economic and political *interests* of each country, which motivate the decisions to pursue these and other initiatives.

In order to draw out a possible foreign policy 'grand vision' for India, I seek to answer what India's strategic interests are and how these would compare to the interests that other world powers—in particular, China and the United States—would seek to pursue. I will also explore the key external factors that will determine India's geopolitical rise in the years to come. Finally, I will try to present a few of my own ideas for what India's grand global vision should include.

Much of what I write here draws from countless conversations and interviews with leading academics, diplomats and journalists over the past few years. I was most fortunate to have enjoyed insightful discussions with officials and diplomats of various countries at the United Nations in New York, with academics at Columbia and outside, and with leading thinkers in New Delhi. Over the last few years, I have had the equally good fortune of having travelled and worked in different parts of the world, in countries at different levels of political and economic development. This has given me—and continues to give me—the very fulfilling opportunity to study and observe social, political and economic life in a variety of contexts: from the democratic world of the United States to the highly centralized systems of the Middle East. My thoughts reflect considerably on these observations, conversations and debates.

Yet, I do not pretend to have the answers to many of the questions I pose. Indeed, I don't even pretend that the grand vision which I present is the best possible narrative for India to follow on the world stage. These are issues to which I believe much of my life ahead will be devoted, and my own thoughts and answers will likely evolve. But the purpose of this book is less to provide big-bang answers and more to analyse the fundamental issues which determine what is good for India, what is good for other world powers, and what is good for the world itself. These are fundamental questions for the foreign policy of *any* emerging power. And India needs to answer them before it is faced with yet another crisis of self-awareness.

FLYING
BLIND

1

The Great Indian Rope Walk

Dilemmas and Delusions in Diplomacy

Circuses were once a grand industry in India. In days that predated the ubiquity of television sets, travelling artistes would enthral crowds in villages and towns all over the country, complete with flame-throwing, lion-taming and trapeze-swinging. But today, India's 130-year-old circus industry is struggling for survival, having been replaced for the most part by non-stop television-broadcast cricket. Once a booming industry, the Indian Circus Federation now has a mere five members on its roster.

My first and only experience with a circus, in fact, was in Moscow. Unlike India, Russia still has a thriving circus industry which has adapted to the new technological age. The Russian artistes did not merely re-enact old tropes; they played new-age music and performed optical illusions, to go with flame-throwing and lion-taming. Yet, arguably the toughest act on show that evening was an old classic: tightrope-walking. No advance in technology could possibly make things easier for you when you're balancing yourself on a thread only a few millimetres thick.

Much as in the circus, tightrope-walking is also the daily work life of diplomacy. Foreign policy is often about maintaining balance between competing inclinations, all the while staying clear of the ground below. Today, there are three broad dilemmas that dominate Indian foreign policy: the first is India's yearning for a broad and international role, which is held back by its visceral focus on the immediate neighbourhood; the second is India's desire to play the role of a rule-shaper on the global stage, which must compete with its reluctance to speak up on sensitive international issues, on which it has long played the role of a fence-sitter; and the third is India's efforts to build a constituency of support as it seeks to emerge as a global leader, which is undermined by inconsistencies in its practice of foreign policy.

Each of these dilemmas presents unique challenges for India's evolution from 'small power' to 'global power'. Many of them don't have easy answers. But no vision for Indian foreign policy can ignore the sensibilities that underlie them.

A Domestic–Foreign Policy

Perhaps the most famous ancient Indian treatise on statecraft is the *Arthashastra*. While some scholars still disagree on its authorship, the *Arthashastra* is most often associated with Chanakya, the prime minister and chief adviser of Chandragupta Maurya, who founded the great Mauryan Empire.[1] By this account, the *Arthashastra* would most likely have been written in the fourth century BC, around the time of the founding of the Mauryan Empire. Many traditions of Indian history believe that the parts of the *Arthashastra* written on statecraft revolved around different bits of Chanakya's advice to Chandragupta Maurya as the latter went about overthrowing his rival, and establishing and consolidating his own empire.

The *Arthashastra*'s views on foreign policy have often been described as 'Machiavellian', but this is only half the story.

Like many Eastern philosophies, the *Arthashastra* also details out the virtues of a good king and the importance of moral authority. Nonetheless, its overwhelming message—at least as might be interpreted in the modern age—is strikingly realist and cynical. The *Arthashastra* assumes the existence of many states and a circle, or ring, of neighbours around any of them (Chanakya calls this a 'mandala'). To any state, its immediate neighbours are the likeliest enemies, and a neighbour's neighbour is a friend—just as an enemy's enemy is a friend. The *Arthashastra* goes on to describe six different ways in which a state may deal with this situation, all in some sense or the other aimed at self-preservation.

But the *Arthashastra* was no manual for 'international' relations. The late Stephen Cohen—an unparalleled authority on South Asian affairs—once wrote that this is a treatise written for *subcontinental* policy, rather than *international* policy. 'Those portions of the *Arthashastra* that deal with statecraft,' he wrote, 'assume cultural and military homogeneity and offer a set of rules for the conduct of statecraft and war. These rules are utterly realistic and rest upon a shared culture and military technology.' To the more internationally minded Western scholar, the usefulness of such a foreign policy doctrine—specific to geography, culture and civilization—might seem doubtful, especially if foreign policy is meant to deal with the outside world. And sure enough, they did not really work with outsiders. 'Indeed, when later dynasties applied Hindu norms and doctrines to invading Greeks, Huns, Scythians, and Muslims, they were devastated,' Cohen goes on to write.[2]

Yet, the *Arthashastra*'s founding principles did guide the course of events within India for centuries to come, *despite* the Greeks, Huns, Scythians and Muslims. In fact, many of the invading tribes ended up being absorbed into the *Arthashastra*'s hard-nosed pragmatism, with little or no regard for national identity or ideology. All foreign policy was conducted with the aim of rational self-preservation and keeping neighbours at bay. Marriage alliances—in

the days of the Gupta Empire and after—served to form a circle
of friends to counter enemy kingdoms. Even the invading Greeks
followed a similar policy of cynical self-preservation when they set
up an empire in western India.

Several centuries later, when the Europeans came to India, local
princes were only too happy to assist the foreigners in decimating
their Indian neighbours. Following the conquests of the French
governor-general François Dupleix in Pondicherry, one local
merchant wrote, 'When [the name of Pondicherry] is uttered, her
enemies tremble, and dare not stir. All this is owing to the ability,
readiness and luck of the present governor, M. Dupleix.' Towards
the end of the eighteenth century, the British began finding luck in
defeating Tipu Sultan and his army in Mysore only by collaborating
with his immediate Indian princely neighbours.

Even at the time of India's independence from the British
Raj, some princes dealt with the new indigenous government in
New Delhi as if it were a subject of foreign relations rather than
of domestic affairs (because, indeed, in the eyes of the nizam of
Hyderabad, the new Indian prime minister and his cabinet were
a foreign government entity, no less foreign than the queen's
government in London).[3]

The *Arthashastra* was written for an India that behaved—and
in many ways, was—a continent within a continent. Since the end
of the third century AD, at no point in time in its history—until
1947—had the modern Indian territory been ruled simultaneously
by less than *four* major independent political entities. And by virtue
of being competitors for power, each of them viewed the other as
a threat.

India's history as a land of countless kingdoms, dynamically
expanding and shrinking, meant that 'foreign policy' did not
traditionally extend any further than the boundaries of the
subcontinent. There are very few examples in Indian history of an
empire stretching beyond the frontiers of the Indian subcontinent,

and where an empire did stretch beyond those frontiers, it certainly did not rule all of modern India. In most major cases, foreign expansion was driven by common folk—not by the king. When the Cholas of south India made their presence felt in the faraway lands of Indonesia and the Malay peninsula, influence was not so much political as it was economic, cultural and religious—driven not by foreign policy decisions taken in the empire's capital, but by the private enterprise of merchants, traders and travellers who took their wares and cultures to distant places.[4]

Independence did not see the end of India's foreign policy introversion. In 1947, India had to weave together some 500 princely states into one independent modern nation-state. Secessionists had to be quelled in the north-east, regionalist sentiments had to be satisfied in the south, and religious and cultural identities had to be reassured in the Punjab.

In many ways, more diplomacy had to be done between states within India than between India and the rest of the world. Think of the river disputes between the southern states of Tamil Nadu and Karnataka, for instance—a legacy of a treaty arrangement signed between the British and their neighbours in Mysore. That water-sharing treaty is more akin to one you would find between two sovereign states on the world stage rather than between provinces in the same country.

Worse for the newly independent government in New Delhi, Partition meant that the subcontinent was still divided between two hostile neighbouring states. To this day, most of India's foreign policy endeavours continue to be hampered by its preoccupation with the neighbourhood and efforts towards keeping external threats from coming in—terrorists from Pakistan, refugees from Bangladesh, and counterfeit money from Nepal.

There were periods during the days of Prime Minister Jawaharlal Nehru when New Delhi tried to play a more outward-looking internationalist foreign policy role. India, in those days, launched the Non-Aligned Movement to counter the ills of the Cold War, declared the famous principles of Panchsheel in the developing world, and even played a role in faraway lands such as Korea and the Congo. In Korea, India attempted diplomatic mediation initially, and then deployed an Indian military force for peacekeeping efforts (a pioneering idea at the time). In the Congo, it led the UN's peacekeeping efforts after civil strife broke out.

But one could argue that these were elements not of *India*'s foreign policy doctrine, but of *Nehru*'s foreign policy doctrine. The Western-educated and internationalist Pandit Nehru, who also occupied the Ministry of External Affairs in his cabinet, often undertook these initiatives unilaterally. Whether they might have taken place if India was ruled by a different prime minister is up for debate. Indeed, after India's defeat in the war with China in 1962, and Nehru's death soon after, New Delhi relapsed into introversion. Nehru's daughter, Indira Gandhi, followed more of a neighbourhood policy than an international policy as prime minister, focusing her efforts largely on the threat from Pakistan. Her son Rajiv Gandhi continued that trend—the highlight of his term being a peacekeeping force in Sri Lanka. And the decade that followed saw too much internal political instability to allow for a paradigm shift in foreign policy.

India views its primary foreign policy objective as the establishment of its own hegemony in South Asia. The driving motivation is national security. These security challenges have not gone away, but they're certainly not as existential as they once used to be. And successive prime ministers have begun to recognize this. Among the earliest to break the shackles was one of India's most revolutionary and iconic leaders—P.V. Narasimha Rao. During his prime ministership, Rao globalized the Indian economy and introduced what he called the 'Look East' policy—an attempt to reorient New Delhi's strategic thinking beyond the immediate neighbourhood and towards East and South East Asia. In recent times, Rao's 'Look East' initiative has formed the cornerstone of India's efforts to build its strategic influence outside the subcontinent. In 2017, India began efforts to sell arms to Vietnam—a genuinely rare gesture for the world's largest arms importer and one of its most insular military powers. It also hosts regular summits with the Association of South East Asian Nations (ASEAN) on issues ranging from political and security cooperation to trade expansion.

Yet, the neighbourhood continues to pose a difficult dilemma for New Delhi as it seeks a role on the world stage. Everybody talks of the hostilities with Pakistan, but India's neighbourhood troubles go much deeper. In recent times, it has failed to act as it would have liked to in defence of democracy in the Maldives; multiple efforts at securing an economic partnership agreement with Sri Lanka have also been stonewalled in Colombo; and perhaps most notably, a crisis over Nepal's newest Constitution has seen Kathmandu seek closer relations with Beijing recently, in open defiance of New Delhi.

Most strategic thinking in India is still focused on the neighbourhood, leaving for little interest, time or energy for the larger world outside. Worse, troubles in the neighbourhood have seriously undermined India's power and influence in several global forums. South Asians rarely stick up for each other on the international stage—and many of India's neighbours have been wary of India's rise as a world power. Their fears are not entirely misplaced: As the largest country in the region, India will inevitably face efforts from within the neighbourhood to balance against its power and influence. But if New Delhi wants to become a global power, it would have to find a way to turn the neighbourhood from a distraction to an asset.

Live and Let Die

One of the great successes of India's foreign policy, even per the critics, is New Delhi's ability to be everybody's friend. India has stood out for its ability to navigate treacherous waters between geopolitical rivals. It somehow maintains cordial bilateral relationships with both sides locked in a dispute, without hurting either side. To this day, India is able to import oil from both Iran and Saudi Arabia, for instance, and arms from both Russia and the United States—sworn enemies pouncing at each other's throats.

What is India's secret sauce? The answer: fence-sitting.

India's traditional approach to foreign policy, since after Jawaharlal Nehru, has been to limit its discourse to bilateral transactions, steering clear of regional geopolitical complications and sensitive political issues. It takes no stance on burning international conflicts in faraway lands, especially during bilateral state visits and high-profile ministerial meetings. From Yemen and Syria to Korea and China, India refuses to offer visions for a solution, or support one side or another in a dispute. It does not involve itself in Saudi Arabia's disputes with Iran, or Qatar's worsening relations with the rest of the Gulf, or power struggles in Venezuela. Africa's civil wars are a planet away. When India does offer its opinion, it mostly presents vague protestations on preserving peace and state sovereignty—words borrowed from Nehru's days as a global peacemaker.

The most glaring example of India's fence-sitting in recent times comes in South East Asia—ironically, the region that received most interest in New Delhi while Prime Minister Narasimha Rao was seeking to break out of India's neighbourhood obsession. In seeking to further expand India's foreign policy activity outside the subcontinent, Prime Minister Modi rebranded Rao's initiatives from 'Look East' to 'Act East', and since 2014, India has signalled its intent to act as an important regional power in South East Asia. In 2015, Modi issued a joint declaration on the region with visiting US President Obama, explicitly referencing the conflict in the South China Sea and calling upon all parties (read, China) to resolve disputes amicably under international law. In light of

India's traditional reticence, Modi's candid talk on the South China Sea was a landmark departure from time-honoured customs—and a welcome paradigm shift in the eyes of many.

Yet, when time came to move from 'looking East' to 'acting East', India found that old habits die hard. The following year, an international tribunal ruled against China in its territorial dispute with the Philippines, in accordance with international law. When China refused to abide by the ruling, India departed from its earlier joint statement with the US and chose not to pass comment—even as Beijing openly disparaged the very international treaty that it had itself chosen to be a party to.* In 2016, when America approached India with a proposal for joint patrols in the South China Sea, New Delhi once again developed cold feet.

It was not until 2019 that India finally joined the US, Japan and the Philippines in a multilateral naval exercise in the South China Sea; but it has always been cautious to balance these out by participating in initiatives with the Chinese as well. The Indian warships which participated in this 2019 exercise, for instance, had also taken part only a few days earlier in a fleet review with—no irony lost—the Chinese. Meanwhile, India continues to be caught in a web of incongruent alliances in the region, having lunch with the Quad (which is America's coalition) and then dinner with the Shanghai Cooperation Organisation (which is promoted by America's rivals—China and Russia).

Forging partnerships with all players in a dispute sounds like a good thing—intuitively. This approach is a key reason for India's ability to steer clear of enemies. But this lack of action is also responsible for a lack of influence. Influence is gained by a rising

---

* The international tribunal was set up under the UNCLOS, or the United Nations Convention on the Law of the Sea. China is a signatory to the treaty, but refuses to recognize several of its provisions in the South China Sea under the pretext of historical claims.

power when it credibly represents—and fulfils—the core interests of various nations, communities, or people. In the absence of such credibility, a rising power will fail to build strategic influence in other countries or secure their cooperation on issues of national interest. With that in mind, think about what happens if a country takes part in military exercises with both sides in a dispute: Neither side can trust that country any longer. At best, that country is no more influential than a by-stander in a street fight; at worst, it is seen by both sides as an unreliable partner—a risk of sabotage.

Some would argue that India's neutrality and silence on sensitive issues allows it the advantage of functioning as an interlocutor, using goodwill on both sides. This was India's greatest trump card in the Nehru days; Nehru's non-alignment during the Cold War often allowed New Delhi to mediate between the two warring sides in various places—most notably in Korea and Vietnam. And India's role as a mediator in various conflicts helped boost its influence around the world—despite its material limitations—by making India an important voice in deciding issues of international security.

But that era is long gone. India is now too large and too powerful to step in the middle of a geopolitical see-saw without making either side wary of its presence. As one senior Indian diplomat put to me at the United Nations, 'India is no Norway.' If India were to mediate in a dispute, it would inevitably hold more sway than a smaller country, and if it mediated without a clear policy stance on the conflict beforehand, both warring parties would doubt its intentions and credibility.

Larger powers mediate more effectively when their policies are clear, coherent and well-known. Think of the United States between Israel, Palestine and the Arab states. For decades, America has been a staunch and indispensable ally of Israel, as well as its largest sponsor by far. Its policies on Palestinian statehood, Arab balance of power and other geopolitical issues in the region are consistent and well-documented. It is hardly what one would call a neutral (or silent) on-looker. Yet, through the 1970s, '80s and '90s, most peace accords in the region came under America's shadow. In the 1970s, Henry Kissinger helped forge ceasefire agreements between Israel, Egypt and Jordan. In the years that followed, President Jimmy Carter's Camp David accords between Israel and Egypt ended a war and produced three Nobel Peace Prizes. In 1993, the Oslo accords were finally operationalized with a landmark handshake between the then Israeli Prime Minister Yitzhak Rabin and Palestine's Yasser Arafat. But the picture could not be completed without Bill Clinton looming in the background.

I once asked a Middle East expert why Palestine has traditionally agreed to American mediation, despite Washington's obvious favouritism and biased interests in the region. The answer, he said, is simple: Palestine knows that only America has sufficient leverage over Israel to make it abide by a treaty.

India's best bet at becoming a credible and effective international mediator today would lie in rebranding New Delhi into what diplomats call a 'problem-solving mediator'—a large and influential power which offers practical solutions to conflicts and uses its weight and leverage to push the peace process forward. The first prerequisite for such a role is a credible policy stance: both parties should know that India represents a set of clear and coherent interests, with a clear and coherent opinion on the debate, and a proven commitment to the pursuit of mutual peace.* Unlike America, India's limited geopolitical interests in different parts of the world today would prove to be an asset by allowing New

---

* Let me clarify—I am not arguing that India should mediate everywhere. Indeed, many geopolitical conflicts are not ready for mediation and settlement, with deeply entrenched interests on both sides that sustain the conflict. However, where a peace process is viable and possible, problem-solving mediation would be India's best possible route. We will explore a solution to this issue in chapter 6.

Delhi to function as an objective and impartial facilitator of peace processes. But that means India needs to take a stance on issues that might matter more to others than to itself.

The Curious Case of Palestine

There is, however, one curious exception to India's traditional reticence, and it comes in Palestine, no less. India was among the earliest and most passionate advocates of Palestinian self-determination, and for years, New Delhi's outspoken stance on the Palestinian issue has stood out as an anomaly in Indian foreign policy.

Over the years, India and Israel have built bilateral ties to previously unforeseen levels of strength. The two countries exchange crucial information on a whole host of issues, ranging from defence and weaponry to agricultural technology and water management. Israel has often supplied India with weapons in times of war. Yet, New Delhi has stuck to its candid talk on Palestine, across governments, domestic ideologies and generations.

In 2011, Prime Minister Manmohan Singh told the United Nations General Assembly (UNGA) that 'India is steadfast in its support for the Palestinian people's struggle for a sovereign, independent, viable and united state of Palestine with East Jerusalem as its capital'. In 2012, India co-sponsored and voted in favour of a UNGA Resolution that enabled Palestine to become an observer state at the UN.

At a Non-Aligned ministerial in September 2017, the then foreign minister, Sushma Swaraj, spoke of India's support to the Palestinian cause as a 'reference point' in its foreign policy. In December that year, India voted in favour of a UNGA resolution criticizing the United States for recognizing Jerusalem as Israel's capital, and called on Israel to end its 'occupation that began in 1967'. Bilateral visits from Modi and Netanyahu to each other's capitals made no difference to India's stance on Palestine. In fact, India's vote in the UNGA on Jerusalem's status came only months after Modi became the first Indian prime minister to visit Israel—an event that was marked by much fanfare in the media.

For India to stick to its line on Palestine is quite extraordinary. Today, India is perhaps Israel's second most important defence partner after the United States. According to the Stockholm International Peace Research Institute, India has accounted for nearly 23 per cent of the total military value of all Israeli arms transferred overseas since 1950. Since 2010, India has accounted for nearly 40 per cent. Israel does not commit to such strong military ties with any other country which shows such committed and bipartisan sympathy for the Palestinian cause.

There could be one of two reasons why Israel will not curtail its defence partnership with India despite New Delhi's consistent and bipartisan policy on Palestine. One, Israel does not believe that India is dangerous enough, because New Delhi will never take any meaningful actions in the Middle East; or two, India is now too big and too lucrative a market for Israeli exporters—*particularly* the defence industry. If the former is Israel's calculation, it would be a big gamble; India is an ambitious emerging power and its foreign policy could become more proactive in the decades to come. But there are good reasons to bet on the latter. In 2017, Israel secured a whopping $2 billion missile sale to India—its biggest ever arms deal at the time. And India's spending trend continues to slope upwards. One study by the Federation of Indian Chambers of Commerce and Industry (FICCI) predicts that India is likely to spend a colossal $620 billion (or almost two times the current Israeli GDP) on defence purchases between 2014 and 2022.

The moral of the story is simple: India *already has* the ability and capacity to take policy stances on burning international issues, without compromising on its bilateral transactions with anybody. Its reticence is less out of compulsion and more out of choice.

To Flip Is to Flop

> It is remarkable that the world order of 1945 dominates global decision-making even today. The architecture of all our major international organizations has remained virtually immune to the momentous political, economic, social and demographic changes of the second half of the twentieth century . . . I believe the time is ripe for the United States to seriously consider the advantages of further enhancing our partnership on major international issues by recognizing India's due place in global councils.[5]

That was Prime Minister Manmohan Singh, delivering one of the most comprehensive speeches on Indian foreign policy since the start of the new millennium. Having just taken office in 2004, Manmohan Singh was making a pitch at an influential think tank in New York for India's quest for global leadership. In the couple of years that followed, the United States signed a landmark nuclear agreement with India. Since then, if there has been one constant in India's foreign policy, it has been the desire for a seat in every assembly and membership in every elite club.

Buoyed by its increasingly lucrative arms import deals and America's dogged support, India managed to find some success in the years that followed, especially in gaining entry into some exclusive weapons control clubs. In 2016, India was admitted into the Missile Technology Control Regime (MTCR) which regulates the export of missile technology; the following year, India entered the Wassenaar Arrangement, another group that regulates weapons exports. These are no small wins, because many weapons control clubs require members to recognize the nuclear Non-proliferation Treaty (NPT); India does not. At the United Nations, India managed to win a few elections and re-elections, notably to the UN Security Council, the UN Human Rights Council and the International Court of Justice.

In large part, India's efforts to garner membership in these groups were greatly aided by its tradition of fence-sitting. Barring China and Pakistan, few countries are as committed to stifling India's efforts, since few countries see India as an immediate threat to them. But membership in these exclusive councils is not by itself a measure of—or an addition to—national power. China, for example, is not a member of the MTCR, while the Nuclear Suppliers Group—which India has tried to be a member of, in vain—counts among its members the likes of Argentina, which, with all due respect, don't qualify as global powers by any definition.

Perhaps the one global council that still holds awe and power is the United Nations Security Council (UNSC). A member of the UNSC is privy to important discussions on international politics and security, particularly when there is an emergency afoot. Each time there is a conflict anywhere in the world, members of the UNSC sit together—in official chambers and coffee shops—to assess intelligence inputs as they come in and to take decisions on the way forward. This means two things: One, a member of the UNSC is able to more easily assess its own national interests during a conflict (by being privy to inside information on the conflict), and two, it is able to voice its concerns at critical points in time in order to influence the decisions of the international community—ranging from sanctions to military interventions.

But being a permanent member of the UNSC is something even more magical. Like a VIP in daily life, a permanent member of the UNSC has several seemingly unconnected privileges within the UN system: Many of them are members of various other UN councils and discussion forums by default, for instance. They also exercise the enigmatic veto—the international politics version of Thor's Hammer. The veto does not just help in preventing the UNSC from taking a decision; it is also an unparalleled bargaining chip. Despite a battered and moribund economy, Russia remains an influential world power, in large part through use of its veto power. In Syria, for instance, Russia has made President Bashar al-Assad eternally dependent on itself by preventing UNSC action through the veto. The veto, therefore, is a significant bargaining chip vis-à-vis allies, and can be used in order to increase a permanent member's foreign policy influence around the world.

It's no surprise, then, that India has long made its aspirations for a permanent UNSC seat the grand prize of its foreign policy pursuits. But this is not going to be so simple. Gaining a permanent UNSC seat is the equivalent of winning each and every singles and doubles title in all four tennis Grand Slams in the same year. It has never been done and it is unlikely to happen. The expansion of the UNSC is a complicated negotiation and the process itself is extremely tedious. Efforts at expansion must fight inertia (of which the UN has plenty) and win difficult majorities. More importantly, pretty much all aspiring candidates have at least one nemesis, some of whom are veto-wielding permanent members who would scuttle their efforts (for India, that includes Pakistan and—quite likely—also China).

But winning a permanent seat in the UNSC isn't meant to be easy. After all, a member who sits permanently on the Security Council has several add-on benefits outside of the Council in global decision-making. No country would campaign for another country to attain such power, unless it is certain that the new permanent member would use that power for its own well-being.

If there is any possible scenario in which this prize can be won by a country, it would be in a world where the UNSC is utterly pointless without counting that nation as its member. In other words, India would have to become so influential and indispensable in international politics that it counts for more than the Security Council as a whole. It would need nothing short of a truly global campaign to get India—or anybody—a permanent seat.

Yet, India does not regard this campaign for leadership and power as being futile at all. Indian leaders speak about it more often than any other leader. Its diplomats take it more seriously than most other aspirants for a permanent seat. Compare the official websites of the Permanent Mission of India and the Permanent Mission of Germany, for instance—while India prominently lists a tab on 'Security Council Reform' in the masthead of its portal, Germany lists it as one of several items under UN reform.

India also recognizes that fence-sitting will not cut it any more. In one of his earliest addresses to senior Indian diplomats less than a year into his term, Prime Minister Modi was as candid and explicit about it as any Indian prime minister could have been. It is time to shed old mindsets, he told the ambassadors. India should position itself in a 'leading role' rather than just a 'balancing [role]'.[6]

Like all good political campaigns, playing a 'leading role' demands that India consistently follows a defined set of policies that reflect the aspirations and interests of the majority of the world's people. That brings us to the third major dilemma in Indian foreign policy: New Delhi is unsure of what it should stand for, and it is even more uncertain about backing up its narrative by walking the talk. Apart from fence-sitting on sensitive international issues, New Delhi is often caught dilly-dallying and flip-flopping.

On the sacred issue of *UN Security Council reform itself*, India has somehow ended up backing two incompatible positions at the same time. As a member of the G-4 along with Germany, Japan and Brazil, India has proposed a compromise on the question of veto powers for new permanent members—agreeing to a non-veto seat for at least fifteen years. Yet, in 2012, India signed a statement along with the more inflexible African states, saying that an expansion of the Council is not possible without veto powers for all new permanent members immediately.

But in no part of the world are the inherent contradictions more evident than in the immediate neighbourhood—ironically, the region that receives the most proactive attention in Indian foreign policy. It is no secret that Pakistan is the ultimate challenge.

Under Prime Minister Modi, India has often been caught confused and paralysed with regard to Pakistan—scheduling talks one day and cancelling them the next. But the trouble extends far beyond just Pakistan. In early 2016, for instance, India had initially issued visas to a group of Chinese dissidents for a controversial conference, before then cancelling those visas for no ostensible reason. In Nepal, India made an explicit show of its disapproval of that country's newly drafted Constitution, after initially pledging not to interfere. Miffed, the Nepali prime minister concluded a historic deal with China, explicitly aimed at reducing Nepal's dependence on India for trade routes and fuel supply.

In previous years, other governments too had their share of U-turns and inconsistencies. In 2011, the democratically elected Maldivian president, Mohamed Nasheed, was overthrown in a coup. Despite early protests against the coup, India was startlingly quick to recognize the new government formed by it. In Myanmar, similarly, India went quickly from proclaiming its support for the democratic movement led by Aung San Suu Kyi to establishing ties with the military junta that had put her under house arrest. And with Sri Lanka, India has often contradicted itself on how it voted in UN Human Rights Council resolutions on alleged war crimes by the Sri Lankan military—sometimes siding with Sri Lanka on keeping international investigators out, and at other times voting in favour of international intervention.[*]

Analysts would give several reasons for these flip-flops. One potential cause is the fear of Chinese influence in the region, which makes India compromise on its own principles. Another cause is that prime ministers often take unilateral decisions influenced by domestic politics, which creates indecisiveness. But whatever the

---

[*] I will give a more detailed explanation of these issues in chapter 3 on South Asia. But for now, the key takeaway is that India tends to flip-flop on various issues.

cause, the larger issue is that there is often an underlying dilemma which forces India to flip-flop. The neighbourhood is the only part of the world where India tries to shed its fence-sitting posture, but each time it cannot follow up its words with action, India's credibility as a regional power takes a hit. An aspiring superpower must stick to its word if it has to be taken seriously. Unpredictable policy choices win no friends and alienate all those who have a stake in the outcome—*even those whom you mean to support.*

If you cannot follow up your policies with action, then the obvious alternative is to take no stand; to sit on the fence. That is the easy way out, but it does nothing to fulfil India's aspirations for global influence. What, then, is the potential solution? The answer begins with self-awareness—an understanding of what India is, what India's interests are, and what India can do for the rest of the world.

2

The India Story

Interests and Imperatives Shaping Foreign Policy

Wise men would often say that knowledge of the self is enlightenment. As the ancient Chinese philosopher Lao Tzu once famously said, 'He who knows others is wise. He who knows himself is enlightened.'

That proverb goes just as well for foreign policy and strategic thinking. If an emerging superpower must gain influence by representing the aspirations of other countries, it must first necessarily understand its own identity, interests and aspirations. Foreign policy must reflect considerably on self-awareness.

One of my favourite parables comes from the teachings of the ancient Indian sage Ramakrishna Paramahansa, who once related the story of a grass-eating tiger. There was once a hungry and pregnant tigress who attacked a herd of goats, the story goes. In chasing the herd, the tigress lost her strength and died giving birth. Left motherless, the little newborn cub was adopted by the goats and grew up in their midst, eating grass and bleating as goats do.

Then, one day, another big tiger came along to attack the herd. Seeing the goats run away, the tiger cub ran along with them, as the preying tiger chased in hot pursuit. Upon finally nailing down the cub, the puzzled tiger asked him why he ran. 'I am a goat and you will eat me,' the cub replied. Amused by the cub's antics, the tiger pulled him along to a nearby pond and showed him his reflection. 'Look at your face,' he said. 'You are the same as me.' The tiger then offered him meat, which the cub relished for the first time in his life.

The Tiger Who Ate Grass

The story of the grass-eating tiger is a fine embodiment of an India that has evolved and transformed at dizzying pace in the last few decades. The grass-eating tiger missed out on meeting his own needs because he harboured an inaccurate idea of himself. A crisis then presented itself in the form of the preying adult tiger. And in response to the crisis, the grass-eating tiger was forced to recalibrate his self-awareness and then act accordingly.

That, in a nutshell, is the story of India's foreign policy since Independence. In the early days of freedom, India was led by the internationalist Prime Minister Nehru. Whatever else one might blame Nehru for, a reticent foreign policy was not one of them. Indeed, if the path to gaining global influence was to represent the interests of other countries, Nehru had put India well on the path to greatness. New Delhi was one of the great capitals of the postcolonial world—its word held great sway in shaping the politics of nations as far away as the Congo and Korea. All that came to be because India was not afraid to speak its mind—and India often spoke words that resonated on the streets of Cairo, Jakarta and even Beijing.

There was but one problem: Nehru overshot himself. India had deep reservoirs of soft power and spiritual strength—the life of Gandhi had inspired freedom fighters around the world, the story of India's independence gave hope to millions elsewhere, and the English-speaking skills of Indian diplomats gave voice to other countries that had suffered colonialism. But these were not sufficient to substitute for India's lack of hard power and material strength.

There are many theories for why China and India went to war in 1962, ranging from Nehru's approval of refuge for the Dalai Lama, to China's internal dynamics which might have tempted Beijing to look for a ready enemy abroad. But one of the more obscure theories put forward was that Mao could no longer stomach the idea of playing second fiddle to a much smaller India.

By 1962, China had discovered newfound belief in its military prowess. Along with the Soviet Union, it had won some significant successes in the Korean War. Mao's China was also much more appreciative of military strength than Nehru's India, and Beijing had deliberately invested more heavily into cultivating its military prowess (never mind famines).

Yet, despite its size and strength, China did indeed often find itself overshadowed in global diplomacy by New Delhi. India had leveraged Western education and the English language to great effect in navigating the speaking clubs of the United Nations. It was also much more imaginative in harnessing its mediation skills in global conflicts, giving it an independent identity (China, on the other hand, was always seen as a lesser communist cousin of the Soviet Union). When the NAM was formed, India dominated its discourse, and it was India's initiatives—such as the Panchsheel—that found favour with the domestic political currents of fellow postcolonial countries. The theory is that Mao went to war with India in order to cut New Delhi down to size and expose the fragility of its national power.

Regardless of the truth of this theory, the massive defeat of 1962 was perhaps the most significant moment in all of India's foreign policy history. Jolted by the realities of its own frailties, India recoiled into an era of introversion and scepticism. For the first time since Independence, strategic thinking shifted from soft power to hard power, and focus returned from the world stage to the regional neighbourhood.

In the Indian psyche, the lesson of 1962 was one of acknowledging the realistic boundaries of Indian national power. New Delhi began to sense that it wasn't ready for an international role. It could no longer focus on faraway conflicts (or worse, it no longer felt that it had the *right* to play a leading role abroad, having been exposed by the army of a fellow developing state).

Nehru's daughter—and his long-time successor as prime minister—Indira Gandhi put these lessons into action during the course of her term: She began to introduce a much stronger focus on rebuilding India's military strength, including through nuclear tests. She also brought the spotlight closer to home, with an almost self-serving and sceptical focus on the neighbourhood, where she defined India's sole interest as the establishment of its own primacy.

In Mrs Gandhi's eyes, the neighbourhood posed myriad existential threats and the sole purpose of Indian foreign policy was to fight those threats, even ruthlessly when needed. In order to do so, Mrs Gandhi also established the need for 'strategic autonomy'—a term that largely dealt with keeping great powers out of the way, so that India did for itself whatever it felt was in its best interests. With the spotlight firmly on South Asia, Mrs Gandhi's foreign policy saw no Indian interests outside the neighbourhood—save when international events had a bearing on Indian interests in South Asia.

In many ways, Mrs Gandhi's foreign policy came far more naturally to India than Nehru's. Over the centuries, the vast land of India—with all its diversity and divisions—had functioned much like a continent, and 'foreign policy' was a largely inward-looking subcontinental phenomenon. Nehru was a pioneer in Indian history insofar as an internationalist outlook in strategic thinking was concerned. Mrs Gandhi merely brought the spotlight *back* to where Indian strategic thinking had for generations lived and worked: the South Asian neighbourhood.

Mrs Gandhi's more sceptical realpolitik approach to foreign policy was also more natural to traditional Indian strategic thinking and statecraft—dating all the way back to Chanakya himself. Her emphasis on hard power calculations and her militaristic approach to diplomacy were a much more honest reflection of medieval politics in the Indian subcontinent than Nehru's preference for cultural influence, soft power and the spoken word. If the tiger ate grass under Nehru, it certainly went back to being its own self under his daughter.

In the aftermath of the 1962 War, Mrs Gandhi's foreign policy corrections were necessary; given multiple famines and crippling poverty, India did not have the energy or the resources for an international role. Instead, the focus was quite rightly on countering immediate threats to national security and, consequently, on building military institutions and resources. It was for all these reasons that Mrs Gandhi's foreign policy doctrine dominates Indian strategic thinking to this day. Indeed, one can firmly make the case that the more influential voice in modern Indian foreign policy is that of Indira Gandhi, not Jawaharlal Nehru.

Yet, much time has passed, and a further examination and recalibration of India's self-awareness is now necessary. Mrs Gandhi oversaw the foreign policy of a small power with a closed economy, limited military resources and a fragile national peace. That India is now long gone—India is now by all measures a great power-in-waiting, with a globalized and progressively open economy, a large international diaspora, and the need for greater influence on international rule-making. As we discussed previously, Indian leaders have already begun to recognize these needs from Indian foreign policy.

What India needs today is a return to the more internationalist approach to foreign policy, with a willingness to once again represent—and fulfil—the needs and aspirations of other countries in the pursuit of global influence. But in doing so, India must be consistent with its *own* needs and aspirations, in order to sustain its efforts credibly enough to win over allies in the long term. It must be cognizant of what it is capable of offering to the world—and what it needs the world to offer it in return. To start with, it has to find a way to articulate and sell the 'India Story' to the world.

Organized Chaos

In the midst of his fight against racial segregation in public buses, Martin Luther King Jr. told a crowd in Brooklyn, New York: 'Christ showed us the way, and Gandhi in India showed it could work.' Until India's civil disobedience movement against the British Raj, King said, few had seen non-violence work in real life as a tool of protest.

Indeed, in many ways, modern India's biggest influence in international politics came through its non-violent struggle for freedom—of which it was a pioneer in world history. When India became free in 1947, it wasn't the oldest major democracy* on earth, but it was the first major democracy to be set up on the pillars of a non-violent movement. Other major democracies such as France and the United States had won their freedom through wars and revolutions, but India was too impoverished and underdeveloped after two centuries of British rule to afford such wars.

---

* Democracy is not a new phenomenon, but for the purposes of this discussion, let's leave aside ancient democracies such as Greece and Rome. The topic of this discussion is the modern nation-state which comes with contemporary complexities, including advancements in weapons technology, tools of communication, geographic size and ethnic diversity, and the obstacles posed by imperialism and colonialism.

It was that last factor—of India's unfancied masses taking on the world's greatest imperial power—that made the Indian freedom struggle such a compelling story for persecuted peoples and nations around the world. The African-Americans did not have the means to wage an armed struggle against their government and survive. South Africa's black population did not have the military power to defeat their heavily armed opponents during the Apartheid. Most oppressed colonial states in Asia and Africa did not have the wealth and resources to wage wars against European armies. But in India's victory, there came a ready template for success for all these nations—no government could rule for long enough a population that refused to be ruled.

When King finally visited India in 1959 after historic breakthroughs in America's civil rights struggle, he told reporters at the airport, 'To other countries I may go as a tourist, but to India I come as a pilgrim.' Several years later, in 2004, when a South African television channel ran a poll on the 'Greatest South Africans' of all time, Mahatma Gandhi was nominated in the top ten.[1]

Even more impressive than India's feat in securing freedom—in the eyes of the rest of the world—was its survival as a stable democracy through the early years. To many political theorists, the idea of an independent Indian republic ticked all the boxes of a project doomed to fail: it was large and diverse, it had already suffered a civil war–like Partition, and most of its voting population could neither read nor write. When the first General Elections took place in 1951, the rest of the world was ablaze: In Indochina, the French were fighting the local Viet-Minh; in Korea, UN forces were repelling communist militias from the North. It was little wonder, then, that the chief of India's Election Commission himself called the polls in 1951 'the biggest experiment in democracy in human history'.[2]

But India's leaders recognized the importance of constitutional rule of law, the separation of powers and independent state institutions to uphold democracy. In a marathon series of debates, the Constituent Assembly put together the world's largest ever Constitution—nearly 400 articles compared to the ten articles that make up the American Constitution. It was far from perfect, like all legal systems in the world, but it instituted widespread faith among the population. More importantly, it granted reasonably lasting legitimacy to India's democracy—a sense of security that the political system is fair and ought not to be overthrown. It created a series of autonomous state institutions—a central bank, a judiciary, a bureaucracy—to safeguard against centralization of power and ensure democratic decision-making. It also guaranteed basic human rights and freedoms (albeit far from perfect and still in need of much reform).

When Jawaharlal Nehru was elected to office as the first Indian prime minister, he upheld these ideals and devoted himself to the constitutional vision. Few observers of international politics put it as aptly as Singapore's Lee Kuan Yew, who called Nehru 'a demagogue who chose not to become a dictator'.

Lee, who was otherwise a staunch critic of Nehru's governance and policies, was not misled in his assessment. As Shashi Tharoor once pointed out, 'Prime Minister Nehru carefully nurtured democratic institutions, paying careful deference to the country's ceremonial Presidency, writing regular letters to the Chief Ministers of India's states explaining his policies, subjecting himself to cross-examination in Parliament by a fractious opposition, taking care not to interfere with the judiciary (on the one occasion where he publicly criticized a judge, he apologized the next day to the individual and to the Chief Justice of India).'[3]

Nehru took especially great care to forge positive relationships with his political opponents and to respect the sanctity of democratic institutions. There are few more telling examples than his equation with Atal Bihari Vajpayee, a leader belonging firmly to the Hindu nationalist camp of Indian politics, who later became prime minister. In 1962, as Chinese forces pillaged the Indian army, Vajpayee called on Nehru and asked him to convene a session of Parliament. Nehru readily agreed. At the Parliament session, days later, Vajpayee tore into Nehru's policies towards China, calling them 'a great sin'. Yet, vociferous differences on matters of policy were readily welcomed by the prime minister. Mesmerized by Vajpayee's eloquence and oration, Nehru once said, 'This young man one day will become the country's prime minister.'

Meanwhile, in Indonesia, Egypt and elsewhere, postcolonial leaders who rode to power on nationalist fervour were quickly constructing centralized authoritarian regimes. Between 1945 and 1950, Indonesia had already had as many as *three* provisional Constitutions; that country's independence was a particularly messy affair, caught amidst the struggle between Japanese and Dutch colonialists in World War II. The first of those documents was a hasty exercise completed in just twenty working days; the drafting body was formed by the Japanese forces, who were forced to retreat towards the end of the war. The resulting document was considered far from perfect—even by President Sukarno himself, who was one of its leading authors—and it had few checks and balances on the executive authority of the president, and minimal protection for the rights and freedoms of the population.[4]

In 1950, however, the Republic of Indonesia was formed based on a provisional Constitution that ushered in liberal democracy. Many of the elements of the 1950 republic would be familiar to Indians: It gave Indonesia a parliamentary system of government, the president (still Sukarno, at the time) had limited executive powers, and there were as many as twenty-eight articles on human rights and freedoms. These included freedom of assembly, expression, movement, protest and—most importantly—religion. However, the Constitution was still only provisional and it stipulated the election of a Constituent Assembly to draw up a permanent document.

In 1955, Indonesia held elections for the Assembly. Yet, the process turned unmanageably acrimonious. An extraordinarily diverse country itself, Indonesia saw uprisings and dissent in several regions, not unlike India in the 1950s. The Constituent Assembly found itself unable to agree on questions of national identity, the role of religion in state affairs, and the federal structure.

By 1956, President Sukarno had begun losing patience with the democratic process. That year, he travelled to China and marvelled at Mao's strong leadership and centralization of power. He mused over China's rise—as he saw it—in sharp contrast to Indonesia's messy and chaotic politics. Sukarno decided that he needed to take matters into his own hands. The provisional constitution had only given him secondary status to the prime minister. But as the then Indonesian foreign minister, Ide Anak Agung, later wrote in his 1973 memoir, Sukarno saw himself as being 'chosen by providence' to lead the people and 'build a new society'.[5]

Sukarno advocated a return to the 1945 provisional Constitution and was vocally supported by the military in his cause. But the Constituent Assembly refused to approve his proposal with the necessary majority. An impasse followed. Finally, in July 1959, Sukarno issued a decree—throwing out the Assembly and reimposing the 1945 document as the official Constitution. Overnight, Sukarno became the de facto military dictator of Indonesia. He was closely acquainted with the loopholes of the law and misused them with impunity. He dissolved the national legislature when it refused to approve his draft budget, subordinated the courts to presidential prerogative, and labelled himself 'President for Life'.

By the time Indonesia was finally able to begin its journey back to democracy in 1998, it had already seen two dictators ruling for close to half a century between them, witnessed two coups that overthrew the two dictators, and suffered a debilitating financial crisis that rendered its currency—the rupiah (Rp)—close to worthless. In fact, it was that last event—the Asian financial crisis of

1998—which proved to be the last straw and unleashed a popular uprising for democratic reform. From July 1997 to June 1998, the Indonesian rupiah lost its value from about Rp 1400 per US dollar to a whopping Rp 16,800 per US dollar, as foreign capital fled.

Yet, by all accounts, Indonesia is in fact one of the rosier stories of political and economic stability in the postcolonial world. It is now even a member of the G20, as one of the twenty leading economies of the world. Most countries in the postcolonial world struggled to institute a stable democratic political system that would oversee a peaceful transition of power on the basis of an election; they suffered autocrats as a matter of routine and saw basic freedoms and liberties as luxuries, even up until the turn of the millennium and beyond. Change in government had to be brought about through coups and revolutions, and the death of presidents resulted in civil wars. This was the common refrain in the developing world—from Chile to Cambodia to Côte d'Ivoire.

As time passed by, India's stability as a modern republic became all the more notable and enviable. Coups were non-existent, institutions were generally respected, and the military kept its distance from politics. Elections took place and voters turned out; mandates were respected and—despite chaos, uprisings and rebellions here and there—the political order of the republic survived. In India's first elections in 1951, as much as 60 per cent of the total electorate came out to vote, thereby reconfirming this legitimacy in the eyes of the people.[6]

India was helped by the fact that its Constitution was comprehensive and its state institutions reasonably well constituted. There was no need for multiple iterations and revolutions, as in other countries. The early generation of political leaders stayed loyal to the democratic spirit. Their experience with British democracy in London (where many of them were educated)—and the presence of legislative assemblies in British India (albeit toothless ones)—also helped; these created a culture of democracy among Indians. The non-violent, non-militaristic nature of the freedom movement oriented the citizenry to respect and value democratic participation and civilian authority—as opposed to military dictatorship and brute force.*

Perhaps even more importantly, the Constitution provided the opportunity for a diverse, multicultural population to express and exhibit several identities—religious, linguistic and cultural— without compromising national unity. This was a form of syncretic, civic nationalism that few postcolonial nations were able to master.

The story of India's political stability and its republic—with all its institutions and paraphernalia—is a significant part of India's national identity. Its success in the early years made for a compelling national story on the world stage—especially given the fact that India was not a developed country and suffered many of the same flaws that the rest of the postcolonial world did. And it gave Nehru tremendous legitimacy, moral authority and soft power in his foreign policy pursuits, as he embarked to be a spokesperson for half the world.

Indian democracy was not pretty—and its politics was certainly chaotic—but it was far from destabilizing or destructive to the basic order of the country. It was chaos, but organized chaos.

What Doesn't Kill You Makes You Stronger

In 1975, there finally came the arguably inevitable challenge to the India Story. That was the year Prime Minister Indira Gandhi decided that she had had enough of the organized chaos. Following a series of political difficulties and a flood of protestors on India's streets, Mrs Gandhi proclaimed Emergency. Overnight, India's

---

* In chapter 6, I will explain why and how democracy often fails in other countries by comparison.

democracy was put in animated suspension—civil liberties were curtailed, political opponents were jailed and Parliament was reduced to a spectator.

This was the moment of truth for Indian democracy. To the rest of the world, it was merely the arrival of the inevitable—India's fragile and complicated republic had finally cracked, and the country took its natural course down the path to dictatorship. It was in keeping with the trends of international postcolonial politics. In the 1950s, Sukarno had turned the idealistic dream of the Indonesian republic into a one-man show. But the 1970s was truly the decade of the dictators: In Chile, Augusto Pinochet had overthrown democracy and established a military junta; in Uganda, Idi Amin reigned with terror; in Cambodia, Pol Pot ran amok. In all these countries, revolutionaries and military commanders had come to power overthrowing the political order, establishing tin-pot dictatorships, clamping down on basic freedoms and imprisoning political opponents.

Even in India, there was a sense of exasperation with the chaos of democracy. In his seminal historical account, *India after Gandhi*, Ramachandra Guha writes that an Indian government official told a visiting American journalist in Delhi in 1975 that only foreigners cared for such things as freedom of expression. 'We are tired of being the workshop of failed democracy,' he said. 'The time has come to exchange some of our vaunted individual rights for some economic development.'[7]

Yet, in 1977, the spiral came to an abrupt end for seemingly no reason—the Emergency was called off and elections were held. In Indonesia, Chile and elsewhere, dictatorships came to a bloody and violent end after decades of tyranny. The walk back to democracy was painful and revolutionary. But in India, the autocratic prime minister relinquished control voluntarily. Even those in power were in some disbelief. When journalist Kuldip Nayar met with the prime minister's powerful son and political heir-apparent,

Sanjay Gandhi, he asked him why the government had decided to hold elections. 'You should address that question to my mother,' Sanjay said. 'In my scheme of things, there were to be no elections for three to four decades.'[8]

The 1977 elections were no sham elections. Both Indira Gandhi and Sanjay Gandhi lost their parliamentary seats; their Congress party was down by a whopping 163 seats in Parliament from the previous election; and the hodgepodge winning coalition together had more than 150 seats above the Congress. The Congress won no seats in India's largest state, Uttar Pradesh, which was also where the Gandhis had their constituencies.

There are many theories for why Mrs Gandhi decided to call off Emergency. Among the more prevalent theories is that the prime minister became discouraged by her image as a dictator and wished to gain legitimacy through the popular vote. Her intelligence services suggested that an election in 1977 would return her to power, and she jumped at the chance. To those who study dictatorships, this would not make much logical sense: When dictators emerge as all-powerful personality cults (as Indira Gandhi did), they generally keep going—for longer than just two years, at any rate. When the odd dictator seeks legitimacy through an election, he typically stages it with a sham election—political opponents still firmly under check, the votes widely manipulated, and important political players bought out. Indira Gandhi's crushing defeat suggests that she failed to do any of this—and her political opponents had in fact already been released from prison months ahead of the polls.

The answer to why Mrs Gandhi's dictatorship fell so soon may well lie in the strength of India's own democratic traditions. Indira Gandhi was an unusual dictator. Unlike Sukarno, Pinochet, Pol Pot or others, she was not the product of a violent revolution or an autocrat with a military background. Her government came to power under a Constitution that she did not attempt to overthrow (even though she altered it during her term). She was also the daughter of an avowed democrat—brought up in the atmosphere of India's republican ideals and steeped, through her personal experiences and interactions, in India's already fairly advanced democratic culture.

Indira Gandhi's relinquishment of authority should go down as one of the most significant events in the post-War world, but what came after was just as significant. The new coalition government made a series of changes to the Indian Constitution, strengthening the power of Parliament and restricting the prime minister's ability to call and prolong Emergency. State institutions such as the Supreme Court also became increasingly assertive in their autonomy.

In a significant way, the experience of Emergency made India's democratic culture even stronger. As much of the rest of the postcolonial world continued its spiral into tyranny, armed rebellion and instability, India grew into an increasingly mature democracy. The image has endured through governments and ideologies. Speaking to Indian and global audiences in multiple locations, Prime Minister Narendra Modi has touted what he calls the 3 Ds of the India Story: 'Democracy, Demand and Demography', referring to the Indian state model which gives its people democratic freedoms, while riding on a demand-driven economy, fuelled by a young and entrepreneurial new generation. He is not the first Indian prime minister to have told that story and he likely will not be the last.

The Second Tryst with Destiny

To most people, Singapore is the answer to every problem. Countless chief ministers and mayors have come and gone across India in recent years, vowing to turn their cities into Singapore. Indeed, Singapore stands out as an extraordinary example in modern economic development. Born out of a bloody and violent race war between the Chinese and the Malays in 1965, Singapore went from being an impoverished fishing village to a modern economic giant—all in just one generation.

The man who oversaw that transformation was Lee Kuan Yew—Singapore's unmatched technocratic statesman and political behemoth for over five decades. Lee was as hard-nosed a pragmatist as any in the world of politics: He approached policy and governance with the emotionless objectivity of a scientist, and had no patience for the ethnic, religious or linguistic passions that dominate the politics of most countries.

It was no surprise then that, as Lee watched India build its chaotic democracy in the 1950s and 1960s, he was highly unimpressed. 'India is a nation of unfulfilled greatness,' he once said. Its society is fractious, its democracy directionless, and its bureaucracy inefficient and inimical to business. For the ideals of democracy, Lee had an especially indifferent attitude. In 1998, he told an interviewer: 'You take a poll of any people. What is it they want? The right to write an editorial as you like? They want homes, medicine, jobs, schools.'[9] To Lee, India's slow-moving democracy was too much of a hindrance for efficient decision-making and the delivery of public services.

It was for all these reasons that Lee publicly supported Indira Gandhi's promulgation of Emergency. In this centralization of power, Lee saw hope for sweeping economic reform and efficient governance. Indeed, the efficient governance did come. While the Western media was critical of Mrs Gandhi's attack on Indian democracy, they too came around to accepting its economic gains. In January 1977, almost two years into Emergency, the *New York Times* observed, 'Now, 19 months later, the Indian economy is better off than it has been in years. Inflation is under control, food is in good supply and the economy is growing at a respectable 5 per cent or so a year.'[10] India's sluggish bureaucracy—Lee Kuan Yew's biggest complaint—was also beaten into efficiency. As legend has it, 'the trains ran on time'.*

Yet, the economic gains were by and large artificial—they did not come from any systemic reform or technological innovation; they came through the iron hand of the state, which forced the bureaucracy to sidestep an inefficient process of bureaucratic oversight and allow big businesses to do their job. Indeed, even through Emergency, Indira Gandhi ran a highly centralized economy with close links to big business. The market economy remained mired in a whole host of laws and regulations that ordinarily paralysed business and employment—the infamous 'Licence Raj', as many call it. It also shut out foreign competition through protectionist trade policies. But those who were close to the prime minister could easily bully the bureaucracy into circumventing the regulatory maze. This was textbook crony capitalism and it led to inefficient monopolies and oligarchies—many of them closely linked to the prime minister's powerful son Sanjay Gandhi.

Crony capitalism almost never leads to sustainable growth, since it does not provide competition or other incentives to big businesses to innovate and increase productivity. Worse, it breeds corruption in the long term—government functionaries would use the bureaucratic maze of licences and laws to extort bribes. If Indira Gandhi did not call off Emergency, the economic gains from that period would have eventually petered out anyway, and potentially led to widespread agitation. That is the way that many socialist dictatorships around the world went, including during the Arab Spring. (Indeed, when the Arab Spring first began in Tunisia, it was not a protest movement for democracy but one against crony capitalism and corruption. On 17 December 2010, Mohamed Bouazizi—a street vendor—set himself ablaze because of repeated

---

*   This legend is true: official records at the Railways show that more than 90 per cent of Indian trains ran on time—a historic high.

harassment from government officials who sought bribes in return for a licence.)

When India finally undertook sweeping economic reform in 1991, it was through democratic change in power and under fragile coalition governments—not through the force of a wise autocrat, as Lee Kuan Yew had imagined. As the economist and author Ankit Mital points out, the reformist zeal began in the late 1980s, post–Indira Gandhi. 'When the V.P. Singh government came to power in December 1989, he wanted to differentiate himself from the Congress,' Mital writes. 'During his time as finance minister to Rajiv Gandhi, Singh had acquired a reputation for being a liberal reformer. The reform process under the Congress government, however, had stalled in the aftermath of the political maelstrom caused by the Bofors scandal, which also resulted in Singh's dismissal as minister in 1987.' When Singh came back as prime minister himself, he picked up where he had left off—and later passed the baton to P.V. Narasimha Rao and Manmohan Singh who rolled out the reforms in 1991 (under another fragile coalition government).

The economic liberalization of 1991 ushered in a new era in the India Story. For decades, while democracy had maintained a certain level of political stability, India's economic frailties perpetuated themselves. Until the 1980s, India's GDP grew at about 3.5 per cent on average each year.[11] Since the reforms of 1991, India has consistently grown at about twice that rate, and the slowest that India grew in any year was in 2008—the year of the global recession—when the annual growth rate fell to just over 3 per cent, according to World Bank data.

The story of India's economic progress since 1991 increased the appeal of its democratic growth model worldwide. Even Lee Kuan Yew was impressed: 'India must make up for much time lost,' he said to an audience in New Delhi in 2005. 'The time has come for India's next tryst with destiny.' To many in the developing world who seek freedom and democracy over stifling authoritarianism, India became welcome proof that even the chaos of an impoverished postcolonial democracy can produce peace and prosperity.

Going, Going and Still Going Global

There was really just one key reason why the 1991 reforms were so successful. They broke down barriers and brought the world to India. In almost every way, the story of India's economic success is the story of globalization. In 1988, India's trade weighed about 13.5 per cent of its GDP. Ten years later, it was as much as 24 per cent. Services trade more than doubled as a percentage of GDP. And not surprisingly, therefore, India's real GDP increased by as much as 70 per cent in those ten years.

Trade and economic openness allowed each country to make use of its strengths, while importing the rest with the resulting gains. To China, multinational firms were offshoring parts of their assembly line—making use of that country's low-wage workers and easy land acquisition policies. China succeeded in becoming the world's factory because these were advantages which no other country could easily replicate. China's workforce was abundant, but the powers of its government were even more so. In his book *The Post-American World*, Fareed Zakaria writes about how Chinese officials once took an American CEO to a site proposed for his new and very large facility. It was central, well-located and met almost all his criteria. But there was one problem: the land was filled with buildings and people. When the CEO pointed this out to his host, the official smiled and said, 'Oh, don't worry, they won't be here in eighteen months.'[12]

Indian democracy, thankfully, does not allow for such forcible government action. But India made use of other advantages. Among the earliest and most visible of the globalization gains in

India was the call centre industry—India's low-skill job-creating equivalent of China's manufacturing sector. The job of answering customer service calls and supporting consumers around the world with technical difficulties was an unattractive one in the US— low-paying and low in prestige. But in India, a new generation of young, English-speaking graduates was more than happy to get on the phone. Since costs of living are lower in India, the salary that American firms were budgeting for these jobs proved to be quite handsome—thereby enabling both the outsourcing firm and the new Indian worker to make healthy profits. For several years, the call centre industry therefore hired hundreds of thousands of workers in India.

The second big boom was information technology (IT). Here, India was unique among developing countries—it boasted a large pool of high-skilled workers who could make use of the dot-com boom through the 1990s. Nehru's heavy investment in technical education institutes in the 1950s and 1960s paid off heavily when the Internet became a thing. As Jack Welch, the late chairman of General Electric, once put it, 'India is a developing country with a developed intellectual capability.' Through the second half of the 1990s, American software and tech firms laid fibre-optic cables under the sea and shipped off back-office IT jobs to India. Here again, the same economics was at play: American firms found it much cheaper to hire Indians over Americans—and Indians found it more profitable to draw salaries from US firms.

India's low costs of living—coupled with a young, tech-savvy, English-speaking pool of graduates—created a thriving services sector that is today worth about half of India's total GDP. In the footsteps of the IT industry, many others followed—across financial services, consulting, retail and so on. The arrival of globalization also spawned demand in the Indian economy, which created a thriving private sector in India by turn. Today, India's fastest-growing export industries are typically high-skill, sophisticated services, such as pharmaceuticals and IT. India is also the largest receiver of foreign remittances, now nearly $80 billion each year, and driven heavily by high-skilled emigrants to the West.

All of these benefits were made possible by international cooperation. Much of India's economic liberalization—which made globalization possible in the first place—came through the sponsorship and policy advocacy of institutions such as the World Bank and the International Monetary Fund (IMF). The IMF was particularly helpful in bailing out India's economy in 1991, when it was on the brink of collapse. International institutions such as the World Trade Organization (WTO) and various UN agencies laid down several standards for policymaking around the world, so as to create a fair playing field for everybody. Meanwhile, America was pushing for the standardization of policy norms across the world, so that companies could outsource work and transact business across countries.*

In 2005, Thomas Friedman documented all of this in what is possibly the most widely read book on globalization: *The World is Flat*. The standardization of Internet protocols such as HTML and HTTP made it possible for everyone everywhere to connect and operate together. The standardization of work-flow software made it possible to outsource work across borders. By signing up to be part of the WTO, countries assured foreign companies that they would be protected by international legal standards, if they invested in their country.

Like many countries, India has a strong economic interest in maintaining and furthering this globalization. Easier immigration is already one of the big objectives of Indian foreign policy: Foreign ministers love talking to Washington about increasing H1B visas for Indian immigrants. But New Delhi needs to push for even more openness across sectors—especially at home. India is still one

---

*   More on this in chapter 5—as well as why India has an interest in maintaining America-led global institutions and norms.

of the most protectionist countries in the world when it comes to trade. According to the Global Trade Alert (GTA) database, India had introduced the second-most number of trade restrictions among all G20 economies between 2016 and 2018 (the highest number belonged to the United States, where President Trump was waging a trade war on multiple fronts). Fears of even more protectionism are now afoot following the COVID-19 pandemic, with Prime Minister Modi's call for an '*Atmanirbhar Bharat*' or 'self-reliant India'.

But given that India's comparative advantages are in high-skilled services, New Delhi should be at the forefront of trade and connectivity on the world stage—even more than China, for that matter. One report in *The Economist* pointed out why, after India sat out the Regional Comprehensive Economic Partnership (RCEP) trade deal: 'Services such as IT tend to be neglected by traditional trade deals [such as RCEP]. Only ambitious, forward-looking agreements venture deeply into these areas, and those deals usually entail a degree of openness to foreign manufacturers that would terrify India's industrialists.'[13] In other words, to create higher-paying job opportunities for its graduates and to boost its exports in high-skilled services, India must push for *more ambitious* trade deals—not less ambitious ones.

More generally, to make use of its economic size and potential as a tool of foreign policy influence, India needs to pursue more openness—both at home and abroad. As I will explain in later chapters, India has a strong interest in strengthening existing international institutions—even those which Indian diplomats detest for being 'Western-dominated'.

Global People, Global Power

People often say that there is an Indian in every country in the world. This is almost literally true: According to the Indian Ministry of External Affairs, there is a person of Indian origin or citizenship in every country or territory in the world—except San Marino, the Vatican and, of course, Pakistan. This is the world's largest diaspora: a whopping 31 million people. If overseas Indians were to constitute a country, they would be the forty-sixth largest member state of the United Nations—more populous than Australia and New Zealand put together.

But what makes India's diaspora particularly unique is the fact that they are influential and politically active in many parts of the world. Indeed, in so many ways, ordinary Indians do more diplomacy for their country than their government does. This is particularly true of Indians in the developed world: According to Pew, Indian-Americans are the highest-earning ethnic group in the US—making almost double the national median in income. At one point in 2014, America had over half a dozen Indian-origin politicians in office—two of them as governors. When Donald Trump became president, he chose a person of Indian origin to represent his administration at the United Nations—ironically, despite his anti-immigrant rhetoric. His successor as president, Joe Biden, now has an Indian-origin vice president.

It is not just America. Indians make up an influential population of over half a million in Australia as well, comprising students, professionals and engineers. In the 2013 federal elections, there were as many as twenty-seven candidates of Indian origin running for office. This is not to mention the Indian diaspora's powerful dominance in South East Asia, Africa, and islands strewn all across the Pacific Ocean and the Caribbean. Over the years, people of Indian origin have served as heads of state or government in over two dozen countries around the world—from Malaysia to Mauritius, and from Singapore to Suriname. As of November 2020, as many as six countries were headed by a person of Indian origin, including countries as far as Guyana and Portugal.

In some of these countries—particularly in Asia, the Pacific and the Caribbean—the Indian diaspora's political influence is for historical reasons; these are leaders who descend from Indians who migrated to their countries generations ago during the British colonial era. But even first-generation Indian migrants are often well-integrated in several countries, and this owes, perhaps, to India's own dizzying diversity. With its wide array of languages and cultures, India forces its people to be naturally multilingual and multicultural even in their home country. According to one *New York Times* report, as many as 250 million Indians—or about a fifth of the total population—speak multiple languages.[14] Many Indians are also fairly fluent in English, making it easier for them to migrate and integrate across the world into foreign cultures.

In recent years, India's diaspora has been an influential foreign policy asset, regardless of who is in power in New Delhi. The landmark India–US nuclear deal, for instance, was aided in Washington by strong political lobbying from the Indian-American community. In 2011, Indians in Australia helped convince the then Australian government to lift a ban on uranium exports to India. In both those countries, Prime Minister Narendra Modi commanded huge rallies, almost as he might do in his home state of Gujarat.

Indians overseas often have strong familial and other roots back home, which give them strong stakes in India's welfare. This strong family culture can sometimes extend to its diaspora even at the highest levels. When Kamala Harris was elected vice president of the United States in 2020, her relatives celebrated with bombast back in her grandfather's village in Tamil Nadu about how their *chitti* (auntie) had won. That same year, New Zealand got its first Indian-origin minister in the form of Priyanca Radhakrishnan—and as soon as that news broke, my grandfather got a phone call from his old childhood friend about how Radhakrishnan's aunt had been their college classmate in the little town of Chittur in Kerala.

With deepening engagement, successive Indian governments have begun to make these ties even stronger. In January each year, an Indian city hosts the Pravasi Bharatiya Divas convention, bringing together influential members of the diaspora to celebrate India's development and the role of overseas Indians in that rise. Each year, the convention's list of invitees reads as a who's-who list of world affairs, across politics, business, academia and beyond—featuring a powerful audience, including prime ministers, presidents, decision-makers, intellectuals and public influencers from around the world. It is a show of foreign policy influence that is truly unique to India.

Champion for Human Rights and Democracy

You might already see a very crucial—but rarely articulated—outcome arising out of this discourse: Democracy around the world makes the Indian diaspora an extraordinarily influential asset for Indian foreign policy. If their adopted homes afford them democratic rights, Indians often organize themselves politically, integrate with the mainstream local population, and rise to power—or, at the very least, influence policy outcomes in their adopted homes through powerful discourse and lobbying. The strength of democracy back home in India is equally crucial: Many Chinese-origin citizens in the West are inimical to Beijing, because several of them fled their country after the Tiananmen protests. But Indians abroad do not share this abhorrence for their own government at home; regardless of whoever is in power in New Delhi, nearly all of them consider the elected government a legitimate entity—and when they are unhappy, they know that India's democratic institutions give them the chance to lobby for change.

The diaspora poses a very strong foreign policy incentive for India to promote true and unadulterated democratic freedom around the world—in truth, a stronger incentive than any incentive that even the United States has ever had or will likely ever have. Think of that landmark India–US nuclear deal. The deal essentially formalized India as a responsible nuclear power, less than ten years after Washington levied sanctions on India *precisely* for going nuclear. That deal shook up the foundations of international nuclear security governance and made India an unparalleled exception in American foreign policy. It isn't unreasonable to argue that such an exception would not have been politically possible in Washington without the active political role and well-respected credentials of the Indian diaspora (and, by consequence, without American democracy).

There are more fundamental political and strategic reasons for India to champion democracy: By virtue of its democracy, India is naturally more likely to enjoy goodwill and influence with democratic governments as opposed to non-democratic ones. This is not just empty camaraderie; it is also a very strategic consideration. As a democratic country, Indian foreign policy and political rhetoric is much more liable to public opinion than, say, Chinese foreign policy. In times past, domestic rhetoric on human rights and democratic freedom has particularly influenced Indian foreign policy in the neighbourhood—in Sri Lanka, for instance, where the cause of Tamil rights has received significant political support from parties in Tamil Nadu. As Indians become more internationalist in their outlook, the strength of humanitarian lobbies in Indian politics will become stronger—and even if the government of the day follows a stoic and Machiavellian approach to international politics, authoritarian leaders know that India's support (or indifference) for their iron-fisted policies could change with each election.

The success of Indian democracy also creates soft-power influence for New Delhi among democracy activists and movements in different parts of the world—of which, in the modern age, there are plenty everywhere, from the Middle East to Africa and South America. India may lose out with authoritarian leaders from time to time, but its democratic credentials—and the story of its freedom struggle—will always appeal to the people in those countries (another fact that autocrats are keenly aware of and wary about). All these factors give India strong reasons to support popular movements which aim for self-determination around the world. In fact, these are also the key considerations that drove India's support for Palestine early on—and it continues to sustain that policy, despite increasingly close ties to Israel.

If all these were not enough, India has a *further* incentive—albeit more obscure—to encourage democracies around the world: free expression of culture and Bollywood. A vibrant film culture can thrive and excel only in countries where cultural expression is not heavily regulated or censored. That has only been more than evident in the success of Bollywood across the democratic world, language being no bar. In 2017, Indian films made a handsome $367 million in box office revenues overseas—more than thrice the previous year.

Just take Germany—a country as far removed as one can imagine from Bombay Hindi. In 2006, Germany got its own Bollywood magazine, printed in the German language. Nasim Khan, its Indo-German owner, told a BBC reporter that Germany's interest in Bollywood began with the screening of the family drama *Kabhi Khushi Kabhie Gham*. 'More than 2 million watched it,' he said. In 2010, when one of the movie's biggest stars, Shah Rukh Khan, visited Berlin, he was mobbed by hundreds of fans who stood in front of the Grand Hyatt, braving the snow and the winter chill.[15]

Such cultural influence is not impossible in less democratic countries—even China, for instance, has increasingly begun taking to Bollywood. Yet, all film industries will attest to the fact that movie-making and film release is not quite as easy in states where freedom of expression is strictly monitored and curtailed. As one Chinese student observed in *Foreign Policy*, China's international cultural influence, for one, has fizzled out, thanks to Beijing's interference. Films, like other forms of cultural expression, work better in open and democratic societies.[16]

Weakness Is Strength

Many critics of democracy would point to China. India and China started out at roughly the same level of development in 1991. But as Fareed Zakaria told me, 'There doesn't seem to be much of a race any more.' Today, China's economy is almost five times that of India's. China is the largest export economy in the world and the second-largest import economy, but India ranks 16th and 11th.[17] India has the highest number of malnourished children in the world; China has all but eliminated poverty. Even on non-economic parameters, the comparison is unflattering. If the 1962 war exposed India's military against China's own might, many would argue that the gap is yet far from closed. As one diplomat put it to me at the United Nations after yet another cross-border attack from Pakistan, 'It is hard to overlook the fact that India still struggles at something as basic as border security.'

But the Chinese one-party development model is a model for nobody. The truth is that China got lucky: Before Deng Xiaoping, China's economy was being burnt down by Mao's communist experiments. If it hadn't been for the good fortune of Deng Xiaoping, China may well have become the modern world's biggest economic disaster and humanitarian catastrophe. Like all things in life, political leadership is a throw of the dice—and in the developing world, there is a higher chance that you end up with Mugabe or Mao Zedong than with Deng or Lee Kuan Yew, for sheer force of personal charisma and political circumstances, if nothing else. But in the absence of democracy, there is limited room for course correction somewhere down the line.

People around the world are starting to realize these truths. For years now, the trend in international politics has been towards democratization rather than away from it. According to Polity IV, before 1990, only 40 per cent of the world's nations were democracies. By the mid-2000s, that figure rose to 60 per cent.* In the age of protestors and social media, people around the world are still asking for more freedom, not less—from Taiwan and Hong Kong to Iran and Lebanon.

India's credentials as a democracy are a great asset in these times—its commitment to democracy serves as a great inspiration to protestors and activists in non-democratic countries everywhere, and its independent election commission, central bank and judiciary are all widely considered to be models for state-building in the developing world. If India can produce sustainable growth and development—of the kind that it did for more than two decades after the 1991 reforms—and prove that democracy can work in the developing world, then the India Story, its policies and its philosophies, will all influence politics around the world.

There is already a unique appeal for the Indian growth model. India's relatively more open society had imbibed the foreign influences of globalization much more readily than other Asian societies—especially China. It created a large, young professional workforce which is fluent in English and easily relates to the rest of the business world. With competition picking up in the economy post-liberalization, India's private corporate sector became more efficient and professional. According to the Bank of International Settlements (BIS), in 2019, India's private sector was under a debt of 56 per cent of GDP. By contrast, China's private sector owed 204 per cent of GDP. But the real problem is in how sustainable those debt levels are: In December that year, Moody's Chief

---

* The Polity data series rates the democratic credentials of countries on a scale of -10 to 10, based on factors such as fairness of elections, political participation and checks on executive authority. A country that scores 6 or above is classified as a 'democracy'. India's score in 2018 was 9.

Economist rated Chinese corporate debt as the 'biggest threat' to the global economy.[18]

The nature of India's economy and politics led to a more services-heavy growth model, particularly in areas such as IT. The result: Across the country, sons and daughters of farmers and labourers became software engineers and programmers. The Indian Space Research Organisation (ISRO)—now a part of space exploration folklore around the world—is the most credible example of this transformation. In recent years, ISRO has put India in an elite club of space superpowers by landing successfully on the moon, putting a satellite in Mars' orbit, and launching a world record 104 satellites on a single rocket. The chairman of the organization, K. Sivan, is the son of a farmer.

Many economists criticize this services-dependent growth model: By its very nature, the services sector creates fewer jobs with higher skill requirements, and it is harder for a country to transition from farming to programming than from farming to manufacturing (and to be sure, even though half of India's GDP comes from the services sector, more than half of the Indian workforce is still engaged in farming). The Chinese model lifted millions out of poverty because it created lower-skilled manufacturing jobs that could easily employ cheap and relatively less educated labour. India missed that bus.

But this is not the 1980s any more. In the age of automation, traditional low-skill manufacturing jobs are already disappearing. There is no point in India—or other developing countries—jumping aboard a train that has already reached its last stop. Instead, they should be investing heavily in quality education to skill their next generation to jump up a few rungs. Increasingly, therefore, people in the developing world too seek higher aspirations. As one young Nigerian scholar put to me at Columbia, 'Nigerians don't want to be factory workers like the Chinese. They want to be doctors and engineers like the Indians.'

There are crucial ingredients which set India up for a potential era of global influence. India's youthful demographics puts it on a possible path towards economic parity with China, as its labour force increases. By 2020, over 44 per cent of all Indians are expected to be younger than twenty-five, according to the United Nations. In China, just under 30 per cent will be as young. By 2040, estimates project that nearly 70 per cent of the Indian population will be working age (aged fifteen to sixty-four). In China by then, almost 30 per cent of the people will be older than sixty.[19]

But the success of the India Story—and its global appeal and usefulness in Indian foreign policy—depends on several factors. The strength and efficacy of its democratic state institutions are paramount. India's democracy is almost solely responsible for its success as an independent nation. Yet, its state institutions still struggle from crippling developmental challenges—corruption, inefficiency, poor governance incentives and so on. For a country that has managed to build nuclear weapons and send a satellite to Mars, basic sanitation and access to drinking water are still huge challenges. In 2019, seven out of the world's ten most polluted cities were found to be in India. India's economy is also desperately in need of reform, lest its demographic dividend turn into a demographic disaster. An Indian government survey in 2019 said that half of India's working-age population was not engaged in any economic activity.[20]

Yet, weakness can also be strength. Most countries in Asia, Africa and Latin America still face these same developmental challenges, and policymakers in these countries relate to the crises that policymakers face in New Delhi every day. It makes India a worthwhile partner in the developmental journey of more than half the world—to share lessons in what works and what doesn't in policy and governance, both for India's own progress and also for that of others. As Syed Akbaruddin, India's articulate and charismatic former ambassador at the United Nations, once said to me, 'India is the world's largest development laboratory.'

Any vision of foreign policy for India should not just keep these domestic developmental challenges and institutional problems in mind—it should also actively seek to find solutions for them. India's foreign policy should also leverage these strengths and weaknesses in the effort to expand India's foreign policy influence. The world needs India to succeed—not just for the fact that its success is useful for the success of democratic movements around the world, but also for the fact that its failure will sink the global economy, for sheer size of its working population and consumer market. This becomes especially crucial in light of China's projected demographic challenges: If China has powered global growth in the last four decades, India is the only country large and young enough to act as the engine of the global economy over the coming four decades.

3

The Tinderbox

Life and Strife in the South Asian Neighbourhood

Welcome to the world's most fearsome neighbourhood. It hosts two nuclear-armed residents, has seen civil wars in at least three countries, and houses the world's oldest, earliest and longest-running United Nations military observer mission. There is a third nuclear power just outside the door, and one of those civil wars ran for as long as three decades. All this is while discounting other nearby countries (hint: Afghanistan) which have been ravaged by multilateral fighting and terrorism for decades.

South Asian countries rarely contain problems within their own borders. Over the years, the region has witnessed cross-border military action on numerous occasions on multiple fronts—from Afghanistan in the north-west to Sri Lanka in the south-east. Domestic troubles often have region-wide implications—and civil wars in one country have killed prime ministers in another. Domestic political interests in provinces of India have often compromised deals and agreements with neighbours. In 2011, India and Bangladesh tried to sign a water-sharing agreement, in a bid to put an end to the long-running dispute over the Teesta River that flows across the two countries. The deal was quickly thwarted by opposition from the state of West Bengal.

Such difficulties have led South Asia to become the least integrated region in the world. In his 1914 poem titled 'Mending Wall', Robert Frost wrote, 'Good fences make good neighbours.' South Asia took him seriously. South Asia is one of the world's fastest-growing regional economies, but that is not because of ties among its members: Trade between South Asian countries is a negligible 5 per cent of the total trade conducted by all South Asian countries (it was 3 per cent in 1990)—and represents just 2 per cent of South Asian GDP. Compare all this with the Association of South East Asian Nations (ASEAN) in South East Asia: Trade within that region is a healthy 25 per cent of all trade by ASEAN countries—and represents more than 20 per cent of ASEAN GDP. With nearly all intra-ASEAN tariffs eliminated, trade grew from $68.7 billion in 1995 to $257 billion in 2017, according to the Asian Development Bank.

But this sort of heavy fencing makes South Asia a problem for India; indeed, it is so critical a problem that New Delhi's plans for global leadership will fall flat if India does not win support in South Asia. Consider this the veto vote over Indian leadership. No global power ever rises if it is constantly putting out fires in its neighbourhood. And the bad news is that it is much easier for India to take action and gain influence as far as Nicaragua or New Zealand than it is to win over its neighbours.

In recent years, South Asia has increasingly become a distraction for India while it seeks to spread its reach further afield in the world. For little gain to anybody in the region, New Delhi's resources of strategic thinking have been drained disproportionately by intractable challenges in the neighbourhood. With every country, there is a headline dispute to which everything else is often held hostage: In Sri Lanka, it is the rights of the Tamil minority and

Indian Tamil fishermen; in Nepal, it is the rights of the Madhesi tribes which populate the Terai plains; in Bangladesh and Pakistan, it is the partitions and their many associated headaches. In all countries, there is of course the big white elephant: Chinese interference to counter-balance Indian hegemony.

Indian diplomats are often frustrated that South Asia is not well-integrated. All large neighbours are always treated as threats by default anywhere in the world. But economic interests often help boost at least economic integration. This is what China has managed to do in East Asia and South East Asia, despite long-running animosity in those regions towards Beijing and even explosive ongoing disputes. The Philippines, for instance, welcomes in Chinese investment on its railroads and highways, even as it locks horns with Beijing in an international tribunal over the South China Sea. Yet, in South Asia, even economic ties are scorned at suspiciously.

Take India and Sri Lanka—arguably the most peaceable pair in South Asia today. India and Sri Lanka have often seemed to be allies so natural that, for several years, they played each other more frequently than any other pair in world cricket. (Cricket is an underrated but important bellwether in South Asian politics. It is the first casualty in India–Pakistan ties following a terrorist attack. But it has also been shockingly useful in nation-building: National success in cricket has often ushered in a new era of confidence and hope—from India to Bangladesh to, most recently, Afghanistan.)

But for several years, they have also struggled to ink agreements for deeper economic integration. Starting in 2005, India and Sri Lanka began negotiating a Comprehensive Economic Partnership Agreement (CEPA), covering trade, investment, technology transfer and other related issues. The draft deal soon ran into trouble in Colombo, owing to fears that Sri Lanka's services sector would collapse under the weight of Indian competition. In 2015, the Sri Lankan prime minister, Ranil Wickremesinghe, was so spooked by uproar in Parliament that he said, 'Our government will never sign the CEPA agreement under any circumstance.'

Instead, Sri Lanka proposed an alternative Economic and Technology Cooperation Agreement (ETCA). But even this deal sparked the same fears in Colombo, where paranoid protectionists said that Indian workers would swarm in and take over the country. In 2016, Sri Lankan prime minister Wickremesinghe said that the two countries would finalise the deal that year. They did not. The following year, India said the same. They still did not. Talks continue to drag on, even as I write this in early 2020.

All Doors Open

It was not always like this. All of South Asia lived as an open society and attracted the world for much of history.* Fascinatingly, social linkages and people exchange took place *independent* of politics. Indeed, empires expanded and shrunk from century to century. Yet, merchants, traders, scholars and monks criss-crossed the subcontinent across changing political boundaries. This is well-documented by several academics. Examining archaeological evidence across South Asia from as early as 500 BC, the University of Chicago's Kathleen Morrison wrote, 'Cities and states in both the Deccan and the far south do appear later than those of the Gangetic plain and, far from representing independent developments, these sites contain indisputable evidence of contact with the states, empires, and religious institutions of the north.'[1]

One of the most telling examples of this cultural exchange across the borders of kingdoms is the spread of the Jain religion centuries ago. Born in the north, Jainism spread down south through the travels of monks and priests into the Deccan. Jain literature talks

---

* As we will see in the next chapter, the story was the exact opposite in China.

of one particular preacher, referred to as Bhadrabahu, who is said to have left the ancient northern kingdom of Magadh some three centuries before Christ, seeking to flee a famine into the south. A sect of Jains is supposed to have travelled across India with Bhadrabahu, eventually leading to the development of regional tongues in the Deccan, founded upon Prakrit—the language in which most Jain teachings were articulated.[2] The travels of Jain monks were later emulated by Hindu and Muslim saints. The Bhakti movement in Hinduism, for instance, is said to have originated in the deep southern state of Tamil Nadu somewhere in the seventh century AD, before spreading up north.

The story of Sri Lanka shows an extension of this kind of people exchange—and even political change—across borders. Nestled in a far-flung corner of South Asia and isolated by water on all sides, Sri Lanka still managed to develop a remarkably diverse population, pulling in from the north and the east. According to Sinhalese tradition and the ancient epic *Mahavamsa*, an Indian prince, Vijaya, settled on the west coast of Sri Lanka some five centuries before Christ—arriving from the northern plains of India. That pulled a generation of north Indian traders down the Indian east coast to Sri Lanka—many of them setting up successful settlements on the island through the trade of natural products. Over time, further waves of migrants came from other parts of India, leading to a syncretic Sinhalese culture composed of both Aryan and Dravidian elements.

The most lasting piece of people exchange, perhaps, is Buddhism. Buddhism was born in India and received royal patronage for export from the Mauryan emperor Ashoka. Ashoka's children—Mahinda and Sanghamitra, both Buddhist monks—are said to have travelled down to Sri Lanka, where their preaching was duly facilitated by the local ruler. Many embraced the new religion and a stupa was built by the Sri Lankan king to facilitate their worship. Today, while Buddhism is the most dominant religion in Sri Lanka, it is all but absent in India.

The exchange of culture, ideas, goods and services across centuries has left South Asian nations today with an odd sense of commonality in their diversity. India in the middle is the key link—and there is a piece of India in each of its neighbouring states (or vice versa): Tamils in Sri Lanka, for instance, Bengalis in Bangladesh, Punjabis in Pakistan and Bihari tribes in Nepal. The existence of such strong cultural ties across political borders should have been reason enough for integration. So, what went wrong?

All Doors Closed

Not unlike the Middle East and Africa, South Asia has been a victim of unnatural political divisions drawn by colonialism. Much of the Middle East's sectarian tensions today are traced back to the arbitrary colonial boundaries which separated the region into unnatural nation-states with no sense of national identity—and no respect for those on the ground. As World War I was coming to an end, the British and the French were busy dividing the spoils of war in the Middle East between them. In 1915, an enigmatic British diplomat in his mid-thirties, Mark Sykes, told the British war cabinet how he would do it. 'I should like to draw a line,' he said, pointing on the map, 'from the "e" in Acre to the last "k" in Kirkuk.' Thus was born the Sykes–Picot agreement which formed the basis of modern-day Syria and Iraq.

The politics behind these borders was driven by colonial interests rather than local sensitivities: Sykes' line was an unnatural border in terms of the fact that it had nothing to do with the tribes and national identities on the ground, but it was not arbitrary to British interests. As one writer pointed out in *Foreign Affairs* in 2016, the line was in fact describing the path the British government had in mind for a pipeline.[3]

In South Asia, colonial interests—both administrative and political—rained down a mesh of lines and boundaries everywhere which affected social harmony. In the state of Assam, for instance, the British imported a large number of Bengali clerks and civil servants to help run the government. The court language and medium of instruction in schools was changed from Assamese to Bengali. It soon led to suspicion and animosity between the less prosperous locals and the more educated outsiders, whom the locals accused of taking their jobs. This is a crisis that runs real to this day, even though both Bengal and Assam are part of India.

Bengal itself has been subjected to multiple partitions—the first of them in 1905. The British viceroy justified his decision in the name of easier administration, but the underlying political consequences soon became clear. Not accidentally, Bengal was so partitioned that West Bengal was Hindu-dominated while East Bengal was Muslim-dominated. That was the beginning of a series of communally motivated decisions from the British Raj—all of which culminated in the infamous Two-Nation Theory, which held that Hindus and Muslims belong in separate nations. Once divisions are drawn and identities are politicized, they lead down a slippery slope with no end. The Muslim state of Pakistan soon found that there were other ways to divide itself—West Pakistan spoke Urdu while East Pakistan (which was nothing more than the erstwhile East Bengal) spoke Bengali. In 1971, East Pakistan broke away to form Bangladesh—the nation of Bengalis. But given that half of Bengal was still in India, it could not even claim to be a nation for all Bengalis.

The arrival of the modern nation-state—with all its colonially drawn boundaries—led to much terror and turmoil in South Asia. The Partition of India and Pakistan is often said to have triggered the largest human migration in world history. In Sri Lanka, Tamils were trapped as a despised minority in a Sinhalese-dominated nation—sparking off a three-decade-long civil war. In the two Bengals, many people continued to live as if they were part of the same state—crossing back and forth between villages that were now in different nations (naturally, this cross-border 'immigration' is a pain point in India–Bangladesh relations).

All this chaos, within and across borders, meant that South Asians felt compelled to draw up the fence to keep each other out. All possible proposals for regional cooperation were subjected by each nation to deep scrutiny. Any deal on any issue is a potential security risk. India is several times larger than its neighbours; naturally, its neighbours are suspicious of anything New Delhi says. But even India itself has not been free of paranoia. In New Delhi's subconscious, each neighbour is a potential enemy, waiting to bring about India's collapse.

Why Won't the Doors Reopen?

The South Asian Association for Regional Cooperation (SAARC) has been hostage to India–Pakistan tiffs. But it's not true that there has been a lack of effort towards integration from everybody else. In 2014, India proposed a SAARC motor vehicles agreement at that organization's annual summit. The deal ran underground very soon, thanks to opposition from Pakistan. But the following year, India, Nepal, Bhutan and Bangladesh got together to sign their own motor agreement to permit passenger and cargo vehicles in each other's territory. In 2019, similarly, India and Nepal inaugurated a cross-border oil pipeline. That same year, Bhutanese cargo travelled to Bangladesh on an Indian river vessel for the first time. Meanwhile, India, Sri Lanka and the Maldives have been exploring their own trilateral maritime security arrangements in the Indian Ocean.

But the problem with all these arrangements is that they are sub-regional rather than region-wide. That has serious implications for diplomacy: It means that in the negotiations for any of these agreements, India is in the room with only two or three of its much smaller neighbours, rather than with all of them together.

The inevitable consequence is that the negotiations seem imbalanced towards India.

Large powers always prefer sitting in a room with two or three other smaller countries, rather than being part of a big ten-nation multilateral negotiation. In the former type of situation, they inevitably have more sway. That is why in the South China Sea disputes, China has consistently proposed bilateral negotiations with each of its neighbours separately. Its rivals, by contrast, prefer a multilateral negotiation involving the whole ASEAN.

Kishore Mahbubani, the charismatic former Singaporean diplomat, once told me how these dynamics were on everybody's mind when the ASEAN itself was being formed in the 1960s. In August 1967, the foreign ministers of Indonesia, Malaysia, Singapore, Thailand and the Philippines came together to sign the Bangkok Declaration, the founding document of the ASEAN. It was not a natural partnership—South East Asia was a minefield in the 1960s. In 1965, Singapore and Malaysia separated from each other, following deadly ethnic riots. Indonesia and Malaysia had been locked in their own confrontation for three long years—from 1963 to 1966. And then there were other complications regarding balance of power. Of the five countries that met that day in Bangkok, Indonesia was by far the largest—three times as populous, with four times as much land area as the next largest country, Thailand. So the Indonesian president, Sukarno, consciously decided not to play a domineering or proactive role in the effort; instead, he allowed the smaller countries to drive the agenda.

Today, the ASEAN has grown to include five more nations: Vietnam, Brunei, Myanmar, Laos and Cambodia. But Indonesia's individual clout on the world stage has grown substantially over the years, and its economy is now more than twice as large as any other ASEAN member state's (the second largest is still Thailand). Yet, nobody thinks of the ASEAN as an organization dominated or hegemonized by Indonesia. Most importantly, no ASEAN member state thinks that.

India's problem is obviously much more complicated. If Indonesia is disproportionately large and powerful, India is so much more than that. Today, India's economy is worth *nine times* the second largest economy in South Asia, Bangladesh. Its geographic position right in the middle of South Asia also means that the other states have limited interaction with each other and cannot easily drive the agenda of integration, even if India yielded them the floor. As one Indian diplomat at the UN asked me, 'What pressing common interests do Bangladesh and the Maldives have with each other without India, that they would want to lead cooperation initiatives on their own?'

The onus to lead integration, therefore, is still on India. In the ideal world, India would find common interests that concern all South Asian nations—and would represent those interests on the world stage by using its relatively higher influence. In other words, South Asians should be convinced that India gives voice to resolving their own private concerns and that they can trust India to represent them globally. Common interest is how the ASEAN overcame deadly riots and deep mistrust in the 1960s: The ASEAN is today known for deep economic integration and trade between its members; but as Mahbubani pointed out to me, economics was not even on the agenda in 1967. Instead, it was the common threat of communism that brought those countries together in those days. India needs to find that headline common interest in its own neighbourhood.

Elephant in the Room

But first, let's talk about India's own behaviour in South Asia. In many ways, New Delhi is its own worst enemy in the region. India has often followed a narcissistic and paranoid approach towards its neighbours, all but casting them as security threats. This is true even of friends who are explicitly called out as 'friends'. India has Friendship Treaties with Nepal and Bhutan. No visas are required for travel to India for Nepali and Bhutanese citizens—and vice versa for Indians. India has also spent money on subsidies for Nepal and Bhutan, particularly on fuel. In the case of Bhutan, the Indian army serves its national defence needs. And Nepalis have served in the Indian army.

Yet, New Delhi has often inserted stifling clauses in the friendship treaties, which have tended to subordinate Nepal and Bhutan to India on matters of security and foreign affairs. Worse, it has also cast them as potential threats to India's security. Neither Nepal nor Bhutan, for instance, are allowed to import any arms or weapons without India's consent. The Bhutan treaty—rewritten in 2007—goes further. On the import of arms by Bhutan, it says, '[This] arrangement shall hold good for all time as long as the Government of India is satisfied that the intentions of the Government of Bhutan are friendly and that there is no danger to India from such importations.' The treaty also explicitly binds Bhutan to the commitment that it shall not use its territory for activities that are considered harmful to India's national security.

The treaty binds India to the same commitment vis-à-vis Bhutan, but in Bhutan's eyes, India is naturally more able—and more likely—to take action against Bhutan if New Delhi is unhappy. By contrast, it is highly unlikely that Bhutan can do anything if it feels that India is using its territory for activities that challenge Bhutanese national security. Bhutan would therefore be justified in believing that this clause was inserted solely for the purpose of allowing India pretext for interference in its affairs, in case New Delhi is satisfied that its national security is threatened.

Words matter in diplomacy—and an explicit treaty obligation that 'one shall not be a threat' can only mean that one is perceived as a threat. In the case of smaller neighbours, such clauses—which are an explicit invitation for interference in their national security decisions—are all the more sensitive and demeaning. In 2018, Nepal asked that the treaty be amended to allow it more independence in the import of arms and ammunition.

The discomfort caused by such interventionist treaty clauses has often resulted in outright paranoia—and compromised India's interests very directly. Innocuous actions from New Delhi have caused much hysteria on the other side of the border. Take Nepal itself. As with most countries in South Asia, India and Nepal too have a contested border strip, and a region which both countries claim to be their own. But for decades, this has been the world's most forgotten border dispute; owing to close social and economic links between the two populations, neither country bothered about it much. All that changed in mid-2020. In May that year, India built a roadway close to the contested region, in order to help pilgrims who make the treacherous trek up to the abode of Siva in Mansarovar. Spooked by India's unilateral activity in the area, Nepal immediately raised alarm—and the episode caused much panic in the Nepali public and media about a potential 'Indian invasion'. Shortly thereafter, the Nepali Parliament unanimously voted to redraw their official map to include the contested region as part of Nepal's own territory. (It didn't help that the Indian army chief scoffed at Kathmandu at the time, saying that the Nepali government was merely acting at China's behest—as if Nepal was a country with no sovereign power of its own.)

As for Bhutan, things have threatened to come to a head just as recently. In 2017, Indian and Chinese forces faced off in the Bhutanese border town of Doklam. India claimed that it was repelling Chinese incursions on behalf of Bhutan, given that India had a treaty obligation to protect Bhutan. Yet, as the standoff wore on, the Bhutanese grew increasingly concerned about becoming a pawn in the India-China power game. In the wake of the standoff, risk management firm ENODO conducted a comprehensive analysis of public opinion in the country. ENODO examined over 25,000 tweets, 351 political cartoons, 127 Facebook Live videos, twenty blogs and twelve magazine covers. The result was telling: about 76 per cent of Bhutanese on Twitter and 65 per cent on Facebook questioned what they saw as their country's over-reliance on Indian diplomatic channels, particularly regarding Bhutan's dealings with China.[4] Soon afterwards, Bhutan made amends by beginning its own talks with China to resolve their border dispute.

Things get worse when India's neighbourhood foreign policy is corrupted by domestic politics (which is almost all the time). Indian politicians often feel compelled to chest-thump at the expense of India's smaller neighbours, all in the name of jingoistic nationalism. And that means projecting India as a sort of 'Middle Kingdom' of South Asia—the fountainhead of South Asia's cultural and civilizational identity. In his critique of the Modi government's efforts to integrate South Asia, Constantino Xavier of Brookings India called this out. 'Cultural and religious values have taken a front seat in [Modi's] Neighbourhood First [policy], which incessantly promotes India as a civilizational hub,' Xavier wrote. 'But emphasising alikeness is often counterproductive with smaller neighbours, where identity politics favour distinctiveness and also fuel anxiety about greater linkages with India.'[5]

This supremacist philosophy drives Indian politicians to say all sorts of unwise but consequential things. In 2015, the Indian army conducted covert operations across the border in Myanmar against separatist insurgents from the north-eastern state of Nagaland. At first, it seemed like a successful initiative—and a mark of cooperation between India and Myanmar. Yet, soon afterwards, the then information minister, Rajyavardhan Rathore, came out to publicly celebrate the prime minister's courage in invading a foreign country. 'This decision was extremely bold in nature,' Rathore said. 'And it involved our Special Forces crossing the border and going deep into another country.' Rathore later made things worse when he was called out; he said that the operation was overt and not covert.

If there is a 'first rule of politics' in the developing world, it is this: No country likes to have foreign forces on its territory. And Myanmar turned out to be no exception. Stung by the chest-thumping in New Delhi, the Myanmar government spoke out, calling on India to 'respect the other country's sovereignty'.

Domestic political compulsions even trigger recklessly snooty policies in New Delhi. The most common pain point in recent times is Hindu nationalism, which has increasingly come to represent Hindu supremacy over Muslims. In late 2019, the Modi government introduced its most controversial policy to date in its pursuit of this supremacist philosophy. That was the Citizenship Amendment Act (CAA), which fast-tracks Indian citizenship for only non-Muslims from Pakistan, Afghanistan and Bangladesh. While the government repeatedly claimed that the law was meant to provide humanitarian support to religiously persecuted groups, the law itself made no mention of 'religious persecution' or any other such grounds. That is because the law could not logically make that claim and stand the scrutiny of a court: After all, there are many Muslim sects such as the Shias and Ahmadiyyas who suffer religious persecution in Pakistan (Ahmadiyyas, for instance, cannot even run their own mosques without fear of attacks).[6] In Bangladesh, rationalist bloggers—some of whom bore Muslim names—were hunted down and killed in years past. The CAA explicitly left all these groups out.

In light of these and other glaring flaws, many believed that the CAA was less about including the religiously persecuted and more about excluding those with Muslim names from these countries. In Afghanistan and Bangladesh—countries that New Delhi claims to be its own key allies—the law was seen as an express message that they were both failed states, all collectively involved in the genocide of their non-Muslim population.

That is a message with very serious political consequences. Ever since India helped them win independence in 1971, Bangladeshi leaders have sought to differentiate their own nationalism from the religious nationalism of Pakistan. After the attacks on rationalist bloggers, Bangladeshi leaders and government institutions have even tried to revive a stronger culture of secularism. In Afghanistan, similarly, leaders have been seeking to build a more inclusive brand of nationalism in a complex and violent environment—often with India's support. The governments of both Presidents Hamid Karzai and Ashraf Ghani have strengthened ties with New Delhi, based on the idea that India and Afghanistan are common sufferers of terrorism emanating from Pakistan.

With the CAA, New Delhi shot itself in the foot: It hyphenated both Bangladesh and Afghanistan with Pakistan, and undermined secular-leaning, pro-India leaders in both countries. Bangladesh prime minister Sheikh Hasina urgently scrambled to revive faith among her people in their country's secular founding values. Dismayed that New Delhi had insulted Bangladeshi nationalism, she said, 'We don't understand why [the Indian government] did it. It was not necessary.'[7] In Afghanistan, former President Karzai was much more pointed and shared his concern that the CAA exacerbated religious identity divisions within Afghanistan: 'We don't have persecuted minorities in Afghanistan,' Karzai told *The Hindu*. 'The whole country is persecuted.'[8]

The spectre of domestic politics has also often pushed New Delhi into dilemmas, leading to inconsistent policymaking, dilly-

---

[*]   If you are Indian and still struggle to see why Bangladeshis and Afghans would be livid with this law, think of this: Imagine that America decided that Indians were collectively involved in the genocide of Muslims because some Muslims were lynched by vigilante mobs and ruling party politicians indulged in anti-Muslim rhetoric. How would Indians feel if America consequently introduced a law which fast-tracked American citizenship only for those with Muslim names from India?

dallying and overall loss of credibility even in the eyes of allies. The longest-running example is in Sri Lanka. Ethnic differences between the majority Sinhalese and the prosperous but less populous Tamil minority sparked a civil war in Sri Lanka in the 1980s. The key belligerents were the Liberation Tigers of Tamil Eelam (LTTE), who sought an independent Tamil state (or *eelam*) in the Tamil-dominated northern and eastern parts of the island. The war ran for three decades, saw an unsuccessful peacekeeping mission from India, and even resulted in the assassination of Prime Minister Rajiv Gandhi. Finally, in 2009, the Sri Lankan army killed the LTTE chief Velupillai Prabhakaran and drew the war to a close.

In the aftermath of the denouement, however, the international community began raising questions over alleged war crimes by the Sri Lankan army during its final push against the LTTE. The matter was raised by the United States and its allies in the United Nations Human Rights Council (UNHRC), where the West asked for an investigation into the war crimes—and foreign intervention in overseeing Sri Lanka's reconciliation process with the Tamils. India was torn: On the one hand, Tamil politicians in Tamil Nadu pressed New Delhi to side with Tamil rights; on the other hand, New Delhi was also eager to win over the Sri Lankan government and seal a proper alliance.

In the end, India swung back and forth like a pendulum, year after year. In 2012 and 2013, India voted against Sri Lanka, but its ambiguity and indecisiveness were quite public up until the last minute. New Delhi was evidently acting in accordance with political pressure from Tamil Nadu—possibly against its own wishes: In 2014, the coalition government in New Delhi lost support from its only political ally from Tamil Nadu, and at the UN that year, India abstained in the vote on Sri Lanka. In Sri Lanka, both the Tamil politicians and the government saw India's indecision and shifting positions in very poor light. To them, any support from India came across as being insincere and opportunistic. (To make matters worse, China was very consistent in its support for the Sri Lankan government.) On the global stage, even humanitarian positions from New Delhi (such as standing up for the Tamils) were seen as being compelled by unsavoury domestic political interests.

The list of inconsistent policymaking in South Asia is long: In the Maldives and Myanmar, India has swung back and forth between supporting democracy activists and juntas/autocrats. In Nepal, after initially swearing not to interfere in that country's Constitution-writing process, India later became publicly upset, because it did not like some of the provisions in that Constitution. In all these cases, India often walked on eggshells, publicly ambiguous on what it was committed to, and trying desperately not to offend anyone (or, worse, trying to please everyone). In the eyes of India's neighbours, the result is clear: It is difficult to trust and be friends with someone if you do not think that they are being sincere in what they say.

Exit, Pursued by a Dragon

It was inevitable that Xi Jinping would bring his global infrastructure investment project to South Asia. This might be a fearsome region, but it is also a rather promising region. South Asia has generally better social indicators than, say, parts of Africa, and a young and ambitious population. And given their own need for snazzy Chinese infrastructure, Sri Lanka, Pakistan, Nepal and others were all very grateful for the Belt and Road Initiative (BRI), just as governments elsewhere had been.

But there were also, of course, political incentives for China's engagement in South Asia. Given deep mistrust and suspicion towards the region's hegemon, India, many South Asians were inclined to pull in China as a counter-balancing force. Xi was only too happy to oblige; under his presidency, Beijing has consistently stuck by the political interests of the ruling regime anywhere in the region—from Myanmar to Sri Lanka and even the Maldives. When a coup takes place (as in the Maldives) and the international community is aghast, China has come to the fore with its political patronage for the new regime. When a painstakingly slow democratic transition takes place with human rights violations in the background (as in Myanmar), China has come to the fore with political cover on the world stage. The more India second-guesses its own policy positions, the more consistent China has been with its own policies.

The entry of BRI to South Asia has been rather unpleasant and confusing for Indian strategic thinkers. At first, India seemed somewhat undecided; it had already joined the China-led Asian Infrastructure Investment Bank (AIIB) as a founding member, but the BRI seemed to have unspoken geopolitical costs hidden under a cloak. Soon, India's fears materialized. In 2015, Xi went to Pakistan on his first state visit to that country and announced a multi-billion dollar agreement for a whole host of infrastructure projects. Among those was a highway that ran through Pakistan-occupied Kashmir—territory which India claims as its own. It was the equivalent of India building a road through Tibet and shaking hands with the Dalai Lama to seal the deal. New Delhi was shocked and raised objections on this overt infringement into its territorial sovereignty.

But things only got worse in the meantime. Soon, China was building ports surrounding India on all three sides—from Myanmar to Sri Lanka and Pakistan. In 2014, a Chinese submarine was reported to have docked in Sri Lanka's Hambantota port, built in the hometown of the then president, Mahinda Rajapaksa.

India has sought to counter China's construction spree with its own projects. In 2017, it proposed purchasing what was called the 'world's emptiest international airport'—also in Hambantota, Sri Lanka—for a whopping $300 million. In 2019, it signed a trilateral deal with Sri Lanka and Japan to develop a port terminal in Colombo. But India has struggled to match up to Chinese implementation. In Myanmar, for instance, India promised to develop ambitious highway projects—yet, these have now been stuck in the mud for as long as two decades.[9]

In recent years, India has been increasingly paranoid about Chinese presence in the region. If there is one clearly articulated and closely preserved objective in all of India's foreign policy, it is that India should be the only omnipresent power in South Asia. But in its quest to build and project influence in the region, New Delhi has ended up pulling Beijing into the ring. In recent years, even outside of BRI, some South Asians have been courting China very aggressively—almost always in response to a dispute with India. In the aftermath of India's quibble with Nepal over the latter's Constitution, the Nepalis started to explore a trade route running through China, in order to reduce their traditional dependence on India for trade. Then, in 2018, as the then chair of the SAARC, Nepal joined Pakistan in exploring a way for China to be part of the association.

Each time, a neighbour has sought to boost ties with China, India has raised alarm. But this has gone as well as one might expect: very badly. India's neighbours already hate subjecting their national security and foreign policy decisions to New Delhi's whims—whether by treaty or otherwise. That is the very rationale for counter-balancing India with China. Each time New Delhi tells the Sri Lankans or the Nepalis not to make deals with the Chinese, it gives them an added reason to make deals with the Chinese.

How to Be a Good Hegemon

Indians often struggle to understand why South Asians are not very friendly towards their government. Sure, New Delhi follows a cynical and Machiavellian approach to its neighbours—and subjects them constantly to scrutiny as national security threats. But this seems the most natural course of action in the minds of many Indians: After all, India *has* faced many threats from its neighbours. Forget Pakistan; India is constantly warding off illegal immigrants from Bangladesh, counterfeit money from Nepal and, until recently, refugees from Sri Lanka. And in New Delhi's eyes, the governments in these countries do not give sufficient importance to these threats to India's security and stability. Worse, they seem somewhat ungrateful for all the good things that India does—from fuel subsidies to heroic rescues in the aftermath of earthquakes (as in Nepal in 2015, for instance). Why court China to counter-balance, New Delhi wonders.

The problem with these arguments is that they assume that India's neighbours are on an equal footing with New Delhi and that, therefore, India is justified in pursuing transactional relationships with its neighbours. In other words, it should be fair—many Indians think—that the neighbours reciprocate equally to India's support. But this is not realistic: Whether New Delhi likes it or not, India's neighbours are not equal to India. Their economies are a small fraction of India's, as is their population, land area and military might. To win the trust of neighbours who are smaller than oneself is hard work—it takes a significant amount of philanthropy from the regional hegemon. Successive Indian governments need to be sincere in the belief that India should give—and give more—in return for little or nothing.

But as irrational as that may seem to foreign policy hawks, it is a worthwhile policy approach. India's global power project needs support from its South Asian neighbours; it *needs* to convince them that a strong and powerful India is in *their* interests; it needs them to see their own welfare in India's security and development. For that, the neighbours must be convinced that India would be willing to share the gains of its growth very generously without asking for subjugation in return. This idea was best articulated by the former Indian prime minister, the late I.K. Gujral. Gujral was a short-serving prime minister; he was in office for less than a year. But on neighbourhood policy, he had remarkable foresight. In recognition of the need to convince India's neighbours that their own welfare would be served by India's rise, he laid down the philanthropic 'Gujral Doctrine'. The first principle of the doctrine, he said, was that 'with the neighbours like Nepal, Bangladesh, Bhutan, Maldives and Sri Lanka, India does not ask for reciprocity but gives all that it can in good faith and trust'.*

Gujral also promised that there would be no interference in the internal affairs of India's neighbours. While New Delhi officially claims that it still follows this policy, it has been severely tested for very obvious reasons. A recurring dilemma for India is on whether to stand up for democracy and human rights in the region (which, for reasons discussed in previous chapters, are in India's interest) or play *realpolitik* by backing the powers-that-be in a neighbouring country. In Sri Lanka, India constantly weighed the need to stand up for Tamil rights with the need to appease the government in power. In the Maldives, in 2011 and 2012, India was torn between answering calls for help from the deposed democratically elected president, Mohamed Nasheed, and accepting the new post-coup regime. In Myanmar, after years of supporting Aung San Suu Kyi's pro-democracy activism, India decided to court the ruling military junta.

In *all* these cases, India has felt inclined to abandon its own deeply held convictions regarding democracy and human rights

---

* Curiously, Gujral's second principle was that same old infamous statement: 'No South Asian country will allow its territory to be used against the interest of another country of the region.' Gujral could have left this unsaid; if his first principle had achieved the reasonable objective that he promised it would, then none of them would have taken the suicidal decision to threaten India's interests anyway.

only for one reason: the fear of Chinese influence in the country in question. Unlike India, China has no moral dilemmas with regards to human rights issues. Far from it, as we will soon see, its political and economic interests dictate that open democracies fail as an idea—and one-party states, like its own, thrive around the world. It has therefore been very consistent in supporting any party that is in power, even if democracy is at risk in that country. Meanwhile, through its dilemmas and dilly-dallying, India has undermined its own credibility in the eyes of its allies in each country, who look to it for pro-democracy leadership.

The good news for India is that this dilemma might solve itself over time, without any need for aggressive interference from New Delhi. The long-term trend in South Asia is very decidedly towards democracy. This is despite coups and crises. Recall the Maldives: In 2011, that country went into a serious political crisis. Their first democratically elected president in thirty years, Mohamed Nasheed, was deposed just three years after winning his election. Worse, the old guard was back in power and was busy strangling democratic institutions. Yet, in 2018, when a fractious presidential election was held under international scrutiny, the incumbent strongman ruler Abdulla Yameen was defeated comprehensively. His rival Ibrahim Solih—a member of Nasheed's Maldivian Democratic Party— was voted president with nearly 60 per cent of the vote. Yameen challenged the results, claiming that ballot papers which had voted for him had 'vanished' and that those planning to vote for him were given pens with 'disappearing ink'. But Yameen found that the judiciary was not very pliant. The Supreme Court's bench of judges unanimously rejected his appeal and castigated him for failing to prove his claims.

Similar stories—of pushback against authoritarianism from other state institutions and democracy activists—have emerged in recent years from Sri Lanka, Nepal and *even* Pakistan. In February 2020, the Chief Justice of the Islamabad High Court threw out a series of sedition cases against Pashtun protestors. 'We don't expect that a democratic government will curb freedom of expression,' he said. 'Everyone's constitutional rights will be protected.'

The wise policy approach for New Delhi, under these circumstances, may be to allow the organic and natural political dynamics in South Asia to take things to their natural conclusion. New Delhi should unequivocally give voice to the democratic aspirations of the South Asian people, without being paranoid about Chinese influence as a result of that policy. That will build credibility for Indian leadership in the eyes of the South Asian people, who categorically seem to favour moving towards freer societies, regardless of political differences. In the event of political crises, India should step in, in support of its democratic allies. In the Maldives, during the 2011–12 crisis, for instance, India should have unequivocally supported Nasheed—even offering him asylum when needed and pushing the post-coup regime to, at the very least, hold free and fair elections at the earliest. Even in the event of Chinese pressure, New Delhi should have held firm; consistent policy is a prerequisite to building trust and influence in foreign countries. While the post-coup regime might have been temporarily predisposed against India, New Delhi would have still won credibility in the eyes of the democracy activists, who held their own sway in Maldivian politics and society.

But general support for democracy apart, India should most definitely desist from subjecting the local policy decisions of a country to its own interests. Recall the friendship treaties with Nepal and Bhutan. The treaty obligation to subject decisions on the import of arms and weapons to New Delhi was a good example of bad diplomacy. If India wants to retain regional primacy in the age of Chinese money, it will have to be much more respectful and charitable to its neighbours—and their distinct national identities— than it has traditionally been.

One Region, One Family

Let me paint you a dream. It is the year 2050. Mistrust and ill-will are gone in a brand-new South Asia. Countries come together to form a South Asian Union. India, as a global power, is the trusted influential voice of the people of South Asia worldwide. There is a South Asian special representative at the UN who consolidates the views and interests of South Asia and articulates them on the world stage; she is helped by India's clout and influence in order to fulfil the interests of Sri Lankans, Bangladeshis, Nepalis and the rest. India's economy is booming, but so are the economies of its neighbours; South Asian students go to state-of-the-art universities in each other's countries; technological innovation takes place across the region. All of this is thanks to cooperative knowledge-sharing across nations and between governments, businesses and academia. Policymakers share lessons and best practices with each other to deliver public services efficiently. Policymaking is done collaboratively and in accordance with a set of enlightened principles, which maintain and strengthen democracy and human rights in South Asia.

It sounds too good to be true, but it isn't impossible. By virtue of being at similar stages of social and economic development, all South Asian nations have similar needs and interests: They need institutional reform to deliver efficient public services to their people; they need trade and investment deals with the rest of the world to leverage their economic advantages; they also need stability and security in the region to ensure growth and development. South Asia is also an incredibly diverse region, and each country has its own unique advantages. In a more economically integrated region, that would lead to significant gains for everybody. But how does India make all this happen?

Apart from following a more charitable and enlightened approach to its neighbours, India has the unique opportunity to make them partners in its own quest for global leadership. That means standing up on the world stage for the interests of its neighbours, even when India itself has no direct stake in the game. At present, however, rarely, if ever, does India organize its foreign policy agenda in a manner that highlights the critical concerns of its neighbours—Sri Lanka's desire to retain ownership over its process of reconciliation with the Tamils, for instance, or the Maldives' concerns over climate change and rising sea levels. Most of these causes are typically delegated to the much larger umbrella of the Non-Aligned Movement, the G-77, or other developing world forums (where, ironically, China tends to involve itself as an organizer). India should instead take up all these causes itself, directly. In addition, New Delhi can even use its relative diplomatic clout to help its neighbours ink more favourable trade deals with the rest of the world.

As the lesson from the ASEAN goes, there is no better way to build trust than by exploiting common interests. India recently launched a South Asia Satellite, which provides communications and real-time weather services to its neighbours. This was a good example of an initiative which exploits common needs. But there is so much more that can be done in a much more institutionalized manner: For instance, a common tourist visa regime for non–South Asian visitors, allowing them to visit all South Asian countries on the same visa, would increase tourist inflow across the region. A visitor to India or the Maldives would also plan trips to Sri Lanka, for instance. Counterterrorism is another fertile area for cooperation, particularly with Bangladesh, Nepal, Sri Lanka, Afghanistan and the Maldives. India already conducts training for police officers in Sri Lanka and has some intelligence collaboration with them. But a region-wide counterterrorism force would not be an unwise proposition. Some sub-regional groups in Africa already have similar forces, which help supplement the national capabilities of member states.

But in launching such efforts, New Delhi needs to cultivate forums that involve almost all its neighbours. It has to allow the smaller partners more of a say on specifics and details—and give them the security of numbers at the table.

Perhaps the most important policy from India's point of view is to increase people-to-people exchange across South Asia. This is vital, because the core element of India's influence, in contrast to Chinese power, is India's potential soft power appeal to citizens in neighbouring states. That requires greater trust and goodwill among people in these countries. That is why South Asians should find it easier to travel to each other's countries than they currently do—and they should especially find it easier to study, work and live in India.

On the education front, the setting up of the South Asian University in Delhi in 2010 was a welcome initiative, which helped attract students from across the region and boosted skill sets and knowledge across countries. More such top-class universities need to be set up in other countries in the neighbourhood—and India should be willing to take on much greater financial and other burdens towards such causes than its neighbours. If India can reintegrate its neighbourhood through the force of its own philanthropy, South Asia will be the better for it. And frankly, the biggest gainer will be India's own global power project.

An Afterthought

I have two confessions to make at this point: First, I have deliberately given Pakistan limited focus and emphasis in this chapter. Second, in the list of cooperative initiatives that I have suggested above, I did not consider Pakistan's participation.

Neither of these was because I harbour any virulent or radical enmity towards the Pakistani people. Rather, the reason for these deliberate decisions is that, as an Indian writer on foreign affairs,

I have become increasingly dismayed by India's fixation on a problem that it will likely never resolve. Richard Gowan, the inimitable British writer and my professor-cum-friend at Columbia, once told me that no conflict can be resolved until it becomes 'ripe'. A conflict is 'ripe' for resolution when both warring parties have more to lose by fighting than they would lose through a compromise for peace. The India–Pakistan conflict is not 'ripe'—and it appears unlikely to ripen for the foreseeable future. There are deep-rooted political interests that keep this conflict alive and make peace deals difficult to sustain. In Pakistan, the intractable power struggle between the military and the civilian politicians sustains the conflict; Pakistan's military would not be as revered in the eyes of its people if it was not fighting existential threats and enemies (perceived and real) on multiple fronts—whether in India or in Afghanistan. This is true even among highly educated and globalized Pakistanis, who may otherwise see benefits to peace with India: To this day, many of them see past military generals—the likes of Zia-ul-Haq and Pervez Musharraf—as blots on Pakistani history. Yet, when asked about the military's political role, they would often shrug their shoulders and ask, 'What other choice do we have? They are the only ones who can uphold stability.' (And let's face it, even in India, jingoism and chest-thumping sell better when there is a caricatured foreign enemy to point fingers at.)

The rest of the world has already resigned itself to these facts. When I asked Fareed Zakaria about India's troubles with Pakistan, he simply sighed, shook his head and said, 'It's unfortunate.'

Yet, Indian strategic thinkers, foreign policy writers and diplomats spend a disproportionate amount of time in thinking about and tackling Pakistan. At its worst, Pakistan has tended to divert precious resources and brainpower away from other foreign policy opportunities—both in the neighbourhood and outside. What's more, India's obsession with security threats from Pakistan has often corrupted its outlook and attitude towards other neighbours; Pakistan is often a key source of the paranoia and cynicism that has been a recurring theme in India's approach to its other neighbours. Remember that infamous clause in India's other treaties, that 'neither country shall allow the use of its territory for activities that threaten the other's interests'? That clause is almost always inserted with one suspicious eye cast towards Islamabad.

Indeed, Indian foreign policy—more generally—often goes through Islamabad. Even at India's mission to the UN in New York, for instance, a considerable amount of time and energy is spent on the futile and pointless effort to demean and isolate Pakistan—an activity which, even when it has succeeded, has brought no meaningful gains to India or its global influence.

That is why I chose to write an entire chapter on South Asia with only passing mention of Pakistan, even though most books on Indian foreign policy would devote entire chapters to Pakistan alone. In doing so, my message is simple: Indian thinkers and policymakers should move on to other more fertile grounds in foreign affairs, which deserve more of their brainpower and energies.

None of this is to downplay the security threat that India faces from Pakistan. The 26/11 attacks were a turning point in the Indian psyche. For over three days, India's financial capital was held at gunpoint by terrorists from Pakistan, who almost certainly had support from somebody within the establishment. But in the aftermath of the attacks, the Indian government found a series of lapses on its own part, which led to the sacking of the then Union home minister, and a number of reforms to the security apparatus (some of which are still pending). The attacks could have been thwarted or prevented had all the cogs in the wheel worked as they should have.

Indeed, many of India's threats from Pakistan can, in fact, be countered more effectively through reformative developmental action at home. In recent times, India has caught a police officer in its own ranks, ferrying dangerous Kashmiri terrorists down towards

Delhi. Shortly afterwards, it apprehended twelve of its own navy sailors for spying on behalf of Pakistan. If India strengthens its own institutions, reviews corruption within its own security apparatus, and follows a more enlightened engagement plan with Kashmiris (which respects their human rights), it would automatically become strong enough to frustrate many of the threats that it faces from Pakistan. These issues deserve books and chapters of their own, but I would not consider them to be part of India's quest for global leadership, as some others might. Instead, I consider these to be domestic issues rather than matters that should dictate a foreign policy strategy. India can take all these steps to become stronger and more resilient without even involving its diplomatic corps. But in doing so, it would transcend the need to think and worry so much about Pakistan.

When President Barack Obama waged a diplomatic war against the Iranian regime, he was quite clear who his enemy was: It was not the Iranians, he said, but their oppressive regime. This distinction between the people and their government was quite critical in helping Obama conclude a nuclear deal with Iran, even though hardliners in that country did not like the deal. It also helped bring moderates into the Iranian government through the sheer force of popular will. When America signed its nuclear deal with Iran, Iranians took to the streets of Tehran to wave American flags.

In its approach towards Pakistan, India should take a leaf out of Obama's book. While the relationship between the Indian and Pakistani governments heats and cools cyclically, India should seek to cultivate stronger cultural and social ties between the people of the two countries. This is vital in gradually fighting against the long-running and widespread anti-India propaganda in Pakistan. Unfortunately, every time ties freeze between India and Pakistan, the first casualty is the most popular cultural element in the two countries: cricket. The embargo on cricket has done little good for India's cause—and lifting it is likely to do little harm to India's cause (even the Indian cricket team may benefit from a few easy wins!). Similar restrictions on Pakistani artists in Bollywood—which crop up from time to time—are also counterproductive. Trade is another fertile area for India to exploit in building trust and leverage among the Pakistani people.

But other more ambitious policies for integration between India and Pakistan are impossible without political will in Islamabad. This is a problem, therefore, which is often out of New Delhi's own control. It is time for Indian strategic thinkers to spend more time on other areas of international affairs where there are reasonable opportunities for gain.

4

The Chinese Dream

The World That China Seeks to Build

In his enthralling book, *On China*, Henry Kissinger—the former US Secretary of State—talks about China's favourite strategy game, *wei qi*: a complicated and intellectually challenging sport that makes chess seem like child's play.[1] With a 19-by-19 grid and a whopping 180 pieces per player, a professional game of wei qi can top over sixteen hours. On average, a wei qi player must consider many more alternatives per move than in chess.

In large part, wei qi's complexity stems from the fact that players start with an empty grid. Players then take turns to place their pieces on the board—each piece having equal powers, unlike in chess. The objective is to build a position of strength by encircling and isolating the opponent's pieces. It is a bit like a game of strategic militarization on an open battlefield—you place your pawns bit by bit anywhere on vast, open and uncontested territory with the aim of fragmenting the opposition army, building spheres of influence and gaining a relative advantage over your opponent.

There are many crucial and fascinating differences between chess and wei qi. Unlike in chess, pieces on a wei qi board do not get into one-on-one action. Instead, good wei qi players must use multiple pieces to gain a relative advantage over an opponent's pawn. A chess player always sees his opponent's army fully deployed on the board and merely needs to guess which piece may move where in the next step. But in wei qi, a player must not only assess his opponent's pieces on the board; he must also anticipate any *new piece* that may be airdropped anywhere on to the field.

There is also a great deal of ambiguity: In chess, a game ends when one player kills the other player's king. Wei qi allows for no such Hollywood-style drama. As Kissinger explains in his book, 'At the end of a well-played game, the board is filled by partially interlocking areas of strength.' Each player has multiple regions of advantage. The margin of overall advantage is therefore often slim, and to the untrained eye, the winner is not always obvious.

It's no coincidence that this game is so revered in China. Wei qi sounds eerily similar to China's approach to the game of global influence. The Chinese do not aim for total victory in a war, as the chess-playing West has often been inclined to do; instead, they bide their time, build their arsenal, and turn up with submarines and military bases in far-flung places where they are least expected. The aim is to weaken the enemy through strategic encirclement and deter pushback. As Sun Tzu famously said, 'The supreme art of war is to subdue the enemy without fighting.'

But China's wei qi–like approach to foreign policy also means the practice of ambiguity—something that vexes policymakers around the world, including in India. China does not articulate its vision of the world in black-and-white terms. It does not seem to believe in total victory or total defeat, in open economies or closed economies, or even in true friends or true foes. In September 2014, President Xi Jinping came visiting Modi's home state of Gujarat. The meeting was one for the cameras of history—full of smiles, swings and sweetness. Yet, almost simultaneously, Indian and Chinese troops were engaged in fierce standoffs along the disputed Himalayan border, after some 200 Chinese soldiers crossed over into territory claimed by India with cranes and bulldozers.

The dichotomy in India–China relations is incredibly stark. On economic and trade issues, Beijing and New Delhi are good friends and often find themselves on the same side of the table—in disputes at the World Trade Organization (WTO), for instance. Yet, on geopolitical issues, China clearly sees India as an enemy to be contained. It practices wei qi–like strategic encirclement (or what India calls the 'String of Pearls').* It has built a highway through Pakistan-controlled Kashmir—the most publicly sensitive insult to India's territorial integrity. And even more notably, it has been willing to stand alone in the UN Security Council in defence of Pakistani policy stances against India. In January 2020, for instance, China sought to introduce a debate in the UNSC on Kashmir, even though all fourteen of the other members were opposed to it.

Why does China see India as a geopolitical foe? To many people, this is because two large neighbours with aspirations for global influence will inevitably clash. That is why Europe was repeatedly in the throes of conflict, until World War II made war infeasible. But that does not explain the whole story. For starters, India and China are far from equal rivals: China's economic weight and military might, by all measures, are still far advanced of India's. Yet, Beijing seems to spend a disproportionate amount of time and effort in poking and shoving India.

---

* The 'String of Pearls' is what New Delhi calls the series of ports and bases that the Chinese have built all around India's borders—from Myanmar in the east, to Sri Lanka in the south and Pakistan in the west. Ostensibly built to benefit the hosting country's trade infrastructure, China has occasionally dropped in a submarine or two at some of these ports.

Order and Stability

China and India are often called 'civilizational states': modern nations that have risen out of thousands of years of civilizational knowledge and an ever-accumulating vault of treasures. But in many ways, China is the mirror image of all that India has ever been. By its very nature, Indian civilization had open borders and coastlines for centuries on end. It invited in the hodgepodge influence of cultures from all and sundry. They all came, ruled and stayed in India—from the Greeks to the Central Asians, the Afghans, the Turks, and finally the British (who were, incidentally, the only ones to be asked to leave). Indian culture, languages, religious practices, society and politics have all learnt and imbibed various elements from the rest of the world.

China, by contrast, has always had a tendency to centralize, unify and homogenize. The Han Chinese empire was among the first in the world to introduce a visa regime, some 2000 years ago. Delegations who visited the Han emperor travelled on fixed itineraries and were issued travel passes—often in such detail as to indicate the exact number of travellers and the towns they were allowed to visit. These were to be presented at multiple checkpoints along their route.[2] There was also economic protectionism. For instance, scholars believe that although China likely discovered paper as early as before the Christian Era, the invention did not quite spread until the Arab conquest of Central Asia some 800 years later—most possibly because the Chinese kept papermaking a secret.[3]

All this insularity means that China has long been a world within itself, rarely influenced by the outside world: Chinese culture and thought have developed more organically and intrinsically than India's hodgepodge nation. A strong and centralized political system has helped: Since at least 1300 AD, Chinese territory has been under the unified and centralized control of only one large dynastic empire or political state at a time—first the Yuan, then the Ming and the Qing, and then finally, the two republics (contrast this to India's political curry of kingdoms). To this day, despite its enormous size and long history, China lacks the sort of dizzying diversity that India has. It has only one major language—Mandarin—and as of 2010, more than 90 per cent of the Chinese population belonged to the Han ethnicity who dominate the eastern part of mainland China (this number might have since decreased, owing to lower fertility rates among the Han and the one-child policy, which was more stringently administered among the Han).

How did successive Chinese emperors and dynasties manage to hold sway for so long, over so vast a land? The story traces back to the sixth century BC—to perhaps the most influential philosopher in Chinese history: Confucius. Born at a time of great political upheaval, Confucius spent much of his life codifying an order for social harmony in China. Like most Eastern philosophies, this included principles of just and ethical rule by the emperor. But unlike Machiavelli or Chanakya, Confucius did not concern himself with strategic affairs to help conquerors consolidate power.

Instead, he drew out a rigorous social hierarchy for China, headlined with the fundamental duty that every individual must 'know thy place'. This was as explicit a statement as possible that order and stability in society superseded any freedoms or liberties that individuals may claim to enjoy. At the pinnacle of the Chinese social order stood the emperor. In Confucian thinking, the Chinese emperor was not just supreme for China alone; he was, as Kissinger puts it, mankind's supreme sovereign—the Emperor of Humanity. 'Chinese protocol insisted on recognizing his overlordship via the *kowtow*—the act of complete prostration.' The emperor was also given the role of being the 'Son of Heaven'—the symbolic intermediary between heaven, earth and humanity—with the duty of establishing social order and harmony on earth.

In the years after the end of political turmoil in China, Confucius' advocacy of order and stability over chaos and liberty naturally won the favours of the new Chinese emperor as he sought to reunify China. The Han dynasty—which ruled China for over 400 years from 206 BC to 220 AD—adopted Confucian thinking as the official state philosophy. In the centuries that followed, each time an emperor consolidated his vast land, the teachings of Confucius were re-emphasized.

Even the Communist Party has sometimes directly or indirectly invoked Confucian teachings. Mao was no fan of Confucius, because he saw Confucian teachings on social hierarchy as the antithesis of a communist cultural revolution. But once the Party established itself, Confucius began trickling back. After the Tiananmen protests, Deng Xiaoping reportedly said, 'Stability overrides everything else.' Under Xi Jinping, the party has taken to Confucius more directly. In 2014, Xi convened a session of the Communist Party elites and emphasized Confucian values at the event.

Even though most of today's Chinese population may not explicitly identify with Confucius, the rigidity of his social order has persisted through the generations and made China a relatively obedient society. To this day, many Chinese value social order over democratic disorder—they would readily forego the freedoms of a chaotic society in order to enjoy the order and discipline of an ordered population. (But, as we will see later, this is not a universal opinion in China; cultural diversity has been a bane.)

Yet, Confucian thinking did not forbid revolutionary feelings. Despite bestowing the emperor with divine characteristics, Confucius did not grant him the divine right to rule. In Confucian thinking, the emperor was to be held accountable for order and stability. If the emperor failed to uphold social harmony and acted in unethical ways, he lost the right to rule—or the 'Mandate of Heaven'. Rebellions would then break out, until a new dynasty restored harmony in the universe.

Wealth and Power

Chinese exceptionalism is the stuff of legend. China's official name in the local language Mandarin is 'Zhongguo', which literally translates to 'Middle State' (or Middle Kingdom). It stems from the ancient Chinese belief that China is the centre of the universe and other states revolve around it. Remember, Confucius had said that the Chinese emperor has the 'Mandate of Heaven' and is the 'Emperor of Humanity'. Chinese philosophy, therefore, has historically had limited patience for foreign ideas. When merchants and traders brought Buddhism to ancient China, they were scoffed at by some Chinese scholars. One influential intellectual, Han Yu, even wrote a scathing account of the imported religious philosophy, saying that it was of 'barbarian origin' and unsuited for the Chinese.*[4]

Such exceptionalism could not be sustained by spiritual force alone. It needed some material backing. And so, Chinese rulers have often striven to give it that backing. In 2013, two China scholars, Orville Schell and John Delury, wrote a seminal book, which identified the central theme that has driven Chinese politics and statecraft for over two millennia. They called it *fuqiang*, or 'wealth and power'. Examining prominent Chinese personalities from the Confucian era to the Qing dynasty and beyond, Schell and Delury point out that Chinese political thought has long been centred around the quest to boost national wealth and power. Any ideology which fulfils the national goal of fuqiang is readily accepted and pursued. Any that compromises that quest must be abandoned.[5]

---

* This was out of no special disrespect to India or the Buddha; the ancient Chinese called anything foreign 'barbarian'. When foreigners came to visit from beyond the Great Wall, the Chinese said, 'The barbarians are here.'

For years, fuqiang was seen to rival the more moralistic and ethical values that Confucius had asked for from the emperor. Indeed, this was a Chinese Machiavellian answer to Confucius. Where Confucianism stressed on moral virtues and a harmonious society, fuqiang prioritized a strong military state, pursuing hard power goals. Schell and Delury found that influential personalities within the Chinese imperial court advocated fuqiang-inspired policies across dynasties.

These voices naturally became more pronounced in the event of foreign aggression. The most testing and turbulent of those periods was the days of the Opium Wars with the British in the nineteenth century—China's first great brush with Western colonialism. After the First Opium War, the Chinese were subjected to the Treaty of Nanjing, which the emperor's court considered unequal and humiliating. A senior official in the Chinese imperial court, Wei Yuan, then released a seminal piece of writing, titled *Records of the Conquest*. 'When the state is rich and powerful, it will be effective,' Wei wrote. 'It deals with the traitors and they will not persist in their ways; it administers revenue and [the revenue] will not be wasted; it acquires weapons and they will not be flawed; it organizes armed forces and the troops will not be understrength. What then is there to fear about barbarians anywhere—what is there to worry about as to defence against aggression?'

Fuqiang has been a greatly useful tool for China's growth and bloom in recent years; it has ingrained in Chinese policymaking a deference for pragmatism over rosy notions of idealism. India's democracy had made wide-ranging economic reforms possible in the 1990s, but India had not pursued democracy because of its possible material benefits. Instead, Indian leaders had followed democracy as an end by itself. To the Chinese, the end is never ideological and the pragmatism of the fuqiang mindset allowed Deng Xiaoping to reform China without overthrowing the regime. When Deng argued for market reforms, he did so as a pragmatist rather than an ideologue. As he told a communist conference in 1962, 'It doesn't matter whether the cat is black or white. As long as it catches mice, it is a good cat.'

It is in many ways a tribute to Chinese pragmatism that a regime which labels itself the 'communist party' embarked upon market reforms. The policy certainly created wealth: China is one of the two great trading powers of the modern world, exporting almost twice as much in 2018 as the world's second largest exporter, the United States. That year, the Chinese economic machine created a trade surplus of almost $360 billion—larger than the entire economic production of countries like Malaysia, Bangladesh and Egypt the same year. There are also other ground-breaking stats: In 1990, China had over 750 million people living below the international poverty line, defined as $1.90 a day (accounting for inflation and price changes). By 2015, it had just 10 million people that poor.[*]

The creation of wealth has been extraordinary, and Xi Jinping is now setting out to build power. China has long believed that its global standing has not been commensurate with the standards of ancient Chinese exceptionalism—befitting the Middle Kingdom of the world. For years, famines and destitution held China back from playing a larger role on the world stage. Deng Xiaoping—known as much for catchy statements as for economic reform—had then famously said, 'Hide your strength, bide your time, never take the lead.' Xi is now done biding his time. In 2013, he unveiled the 'Chinese Dream'—a quest for 'the great rejuvenation of the Chinese nation'. As the state-run *China Daily* said, 'In the global prospect, the Chinese Dream will change the global landscape, which was shaped by Western countries over the past two centuries during industrialization.'[6]

In recent years, when China has found itself unable to have a respectable enough seat at the table, it has simply gone away

---

[*]   All these numbers are from the World Bank.

to buy its own new table: It founded the Asian Infrastructure Investment Bank (AIIB) in 2015 in response to its inability to acquire a bigger voice at the World Bank. With the rest of the BRICS (Brazil, Russia, India and South Africa) nations, it founded the New Development Bank in 2014. When the Obama administration snubbed it by excluding it from the Trans-Pacific Partnership (TPP) trade deal, China launched its own counter-deal—the Regional Comprehensive Economic Partnership (RCEP).

Closer to home, Xi has brought back some of ancient China's snobbish exceptionalism in his approach to Beijing's neighbours. In the ancient era, China's neighbours used to pay tributes to the Chinese emperor—the 'Emperor of Humanity'. Xi now wants to revive Chinese dominance in its neighbourhood as part of his Chinese Dream, and he is accordingly stamping his authority everywhere. The South China Sea has been a disputed water body in Asia for several years. Yet, under Xi, China has escalated things: Xi has been militarizing the South China Sea indiscriminately and pushing at neighbours more aggressively. China has sprung up at random places in the sea, building islands that didn't previously exist and putting weapons on them.[7] In 2016, when an international tribunal ruled in favour of the Philippines in the South China Sea dispute, China rejected the ruling outright. With India, border skirmishes have picked up on and off—peaking with the standoff in Ladakh, in 2020, which resulted in bullets being fired for the first time since 1962.

Xi has followed a carrot-and-stick approach towards his neighbours—luring them with shiny new railway projects and highway contracts, while occasionally showcasing China's military might to show them who is boss. But there can be no mistaking the fact that, under Xi, China has followed a decidedly more muscular approach—and has consciously sought to project power in the neighbourhood.

A lot of this should also be seen as arising out of domestic politics. Indeed, in the absence of electoral mandates, rulers across Chinese history have often pursued fuqiang only to win legitimacy in the eyes of their people. Confucius said that a ruler who failed to uphold social harmony would stand to lose his right to rule—sparking a justifiable revolution. But just as much, a ruler who is unable to create wealth and power for the great Chinese nation would also be considered unworthy of ruling China. Mao failed and his doctrines were quickly junked. Xi does not want his Chinese Dream to fail—and that means that he needs to reaffirm his own legitimacy by creating wealth and power for modern China (or, at the very least, the illusion of wealth and power).

What Can't Money Buy?

Think about our theory from earlier: The path to global power is to represent the interests of other countries, but in a manner that is consistent with your own interests. In other words, you do for others what you are *able* to do; and you do for others what is good for *both* of you. Xi's foreign policy lives and breathes this theory worldwide.

In the Chinese economic success model, trade and investment are everything. The Chinese are especially obsessed with investment in infrastructure—arguably their best skill and asset. In shockingly quick time, Chinese cities have transformed themselves, built on the back of trade surplus money, cheap construction labour and heavy lending. In 2013, Reuters photographer Carlos Berria published two images of the Shanghai skyline, twenty-six years apart from each other. The transformation was breathtaking enough to make it to all over the international press. In 1987, Shanghai's financial district of Pudong was no more than a little swamp on the east China coast.

By 2013, the same area was packed with skyscrapers, rivalling downtown Manhattan and boasting the world's second tallest tower—the Shanghai Tower—standing 125 stories high.

Infrastructure is more important to the Chinese economy than most people realize on the outside. China's economy is more dependent on investment spending than any other major economy in the world: In 2017, as much as 45 per cent of China's GDP came through investment. More than a fifth of that came from out of investment in infrastructure. With an ageing population and rising wages, the trend for the manufacturing sector has been downward. But the infrastructure sector is still expanding, in terms of share of the GDP.[8] There is an obsession with world records too—not atypical of centralized authoritarian regimes. Over the years, China has built the world's highest railway, largest hydropower project, and biggest water transfer system. A running theme is to keep besting its own records.*

But China's infrastructure mania has lasted long beyond its utility. In the mountainous Hunan province of southern China, a few years ago, there arose the splendid Chishi Bridge— another dazzling infrastructure project on China's long and enviable list. Meant to connect the mountainous southern parts of the country with the prosperous east coast, the bridge cost some $300 million and ran over two kilometres long. The local government had borrowed heavily from state-owned Chinese banks in order to finance the project. But as it soon realized, none of the farmers in the area were willing to pay to use the expressway. The project soon ran into debt, leaving provincial officials tied up.

---

* The Chinese are now passing on this tradition to the oil-rich Gulf states. As I write these words, Jeddah's under-construction Kingdom Tower is trying to climb up beyond Dubai's Burj Khalifa for the tag of the world's tallest skyscraper.

Projects such as the Chishi Bridge have helped push China's government debt to 73 per cent of GDP, according to the IMF. In the Guizhou province—the worst hit—debt flew as high as 170 per cent by 2018. Household numbers are no better: With heavy investment in swanky new 'ghost towns' where no one seems to want to live, Chinese households have racked up a whopping $6.8 trillion in debt.[9]

High debt levels have forced Beijing to start tightening the screws on infrastructure spending at home, leading to a slowdown in economic growth. But Xi Jinping saw an opportunity in the mess: Much of the developing world languishes in poor infrastructure and admires China's snazzy steel structures. So, if the Chinese can't build in China, why shouldn't they build around the world? That was the genesis of the massive Silk Road project—also known as the Belt and Road Initiative.

In 2013, during state visits to Indonesia and Kazakhstan, Xi launched his grand foreign policy vision to take China's infrastructure-building prowess to the world. It rode on China's history as a major destination for traders along the ancient silk route, running from East Asia to Europe. Xi's plan was to develop highways, railways and maritime ports all across Asia and parts of Africa, involving more than 60 countries and covering two-thirds of humanity. China is supposed to have already spent around $200 billion on BRI projects around the world—from Djibouti to the Philippines—and according to Morgan Stanley, it could spend more than $1 trillion by 2027.[10]

Even outside of BRI, China has been investing heavily in other kinds of infrastructure—from stadiums to hospitals—all over the developing world. According to an Ernst and Young report, between 2014 and 2018, China was the biggest source of FDI in Africa by far, and Chinese investment created more than twice as many jobs as investment from the US.[11]

But this is not free money. Most BRI and other Chinese projects are financed—not through aid—but through low-interest loans from Chinese banks, granted to the receiving country, to pay mostly Chinese firms, employing largely Chinese labour. In some cases, Chinese assistance is paid back by the foreign government in ways other than a direct reimbursement of money—often giving Beijing outsized influence in that country.

Take Angola, an oil-rich country in southwestern Africa. From 2004 to 2010, Angola received $10.5 billion of credit from China's Eximbank. These subsidized loans were tied to the use of Chinese companies to undertake 70 per cent of the country's construction and civil engineering contracts and were to be repaid through commodity exports back to China. At the same time, the Chinese Eximbank also announced a $2 billion loan to finance Angola's infrastructure reconstruction, and Chinese companies duly increased their investments in Angola. The China Petroleum and Chemical Corporation (Sinopec) acquired majority ownership of several oil blocks and formed a joint venture with Sonangol, Angola's national oil company. The result: Since 2007, Angola has been one of China's top trading partners in Africa, and its oil reserves are heavily dependent on Chinese support.

When Indians or Americans invest in a foreign country, it is done mostly through private enterprises and private money. Governments have little say. But Chinese investment is a government-to-government deal. In Africa, for instance, more than three-quarters of all Chinese investment comes from central state-owned enterprises, and even the rest is largely by firms owned by provincial governments, or firms partly owned by the state. The domination of Chinese investment by state-owned enterprises is significant. It means that Beijing is able to use these deals much more strategically than other countries. If India's potent foreign policy asset is its diaspora, China's equivalent is that which has enticed mankind ever since its invention: money.

What Money Can't Buy

Xi's export of China's infrastructure capacity has sometimes been welcomed in developing countries around the world. I have heard countless stories from friends in Colombia, Kenya and Tunisia, who narrate how the fruits of China's rise arrived at their doorstep in the form of state-of-the-art highways or power grids. But it hasn't all been rosy. The Chinese-ness of Chinese assistance—financed by Chinese banks, built by Chinese firms, constructed by Chinese labour, and paid for through Chinese influence—has irked recipients in some parts of the world.

In 2018, Sri Lanka was reported to owe China a whopping $13 billion. Politicians in Colombo had long been cribbing about Chinese 'neo-colonialism'. Three years earlier, President Sirisena had come to power riding that same anti-Chinese wave against strongman incumbent Mahinda Rajapaksa. Having won office, Sirisena now sought to renegotiate the deal with the Chinese. But Beijing did not give in so easily. In the end, Sirisena had to walk away having sold 70 per cent of the stake in a Chinese-constructed port back to the Chinese. That only further angered the public, and difficulties continue to plague the relationship. In 2020, Rajapaksa and his brother returned to power in Colombo, but this time, the brothers promised that they would be far less subservient to China than during Rajapaksa's previous stint.

Similar challenges have risen in other countries. Like Sirisena, Mahathir Mohamad came back to power in Malaysia in 2018 excoriating China's 'overpriced' investments. Once in office, he cancelled $22 billion worth of BRI projects. In Pakistan—China's closest ally in South Asia—the new prime minister, Imran Khan, started seeking assistance from Saudi Arabia and the IMF to diversify

away from the heavy debt that his country owes the Chinese.*
Even in Africa, where people have traditionally had largely positive
views of China, Chinese investments have increasingly come under
fire. In Egypt—the fifth-largest recipient of Chinese investment
in Africa—only 38 per cent of the people rated Chinese influence
as being at least somewhat positive, in the 2014 Afrobarometer
survey.[12] In Sudan's troubled Darfur region some years ago, anti-
government militants abducted Chinese workers. Years earlier,
ethnic rebels ambushed a Chinese-run oilfield in Ethiopia,
killing seventy.[13] In Zambia, Chinese properties and people have
repeatedly come under attack.

The challenges posed by democracy or popular protests have
influenced the countries where Beijing invests. In 2015, a Chinese
expert at Brookings, David Dollar, documented this in a remarkable
comparison between investments by the Chinese and those by
other countries. While most foreign firms preferred to invest in
countries with a strong record in rule of law and property rights—
generally characteristics shared by states with stable democratic
institutions—Chinese firms were largely indifferent to either of
these attributes. Instead, China preferred to invest in countries
with strong political stability, even if they had weak governance
records or low transparency. These included the likes of Venezuela
(under Hugo Chavez), Ecuador, Egypt, Sudan, Cambodia and
Zimbabwe.[14]

The chaotic uncertainty and multi-stakeholder decision-
making process of democratic countries confounds the Chinese.
If the public is suspicious of Chinese loans and Chinese labour in
their countries, then Beijing could simply bypass them by using
its money and muscle to coerce the government in charge. But
that does not work in democracies. In a democracy, governments

---

* This relationship will sustain itself though, due to their problems
with India.

change, policies evolve, and public opinion is supreme. Today's deal could be scrapped tomorrow by a Mahathir or a Sirisena.

Spooked by the vagaries of democracy, Beijing has often had to take pro-authoritarian stances in countries struggling through a democratic transition. In Egypt, for instance, China has supported clampdowns on liberty by Egyptian president Abdel Fattah el-Sisi, mostly in the name of protecting 'state sovereignty'. Elsewhere, it has had a vested interest in ensuring the stability of a dictator, despite popular dissent—as with Omar al-Bashir in Sudan.[15] The world often talks about the Russians or the Chinese throwing their weight behind dictators—but it rarely ever recognizes the economic interests that often go behind that.

Exporting the Chinese Dream

If communism could have ever succeeded, it would have had to be under the Soviets. The Soviet Union was a true global superpower. In a matter of three decades, Soviet leaders took an impoverished agrarian basket case and turned it into a major industrial power. While America languished under the Great Depression, the Soviet Union was transforming itself at a rapid pace. After World War II, the Soviets continued to press on: From the mid-1960s to the mid-1970s, the Soviet economy grew faster on average than the US economy. The Soviet Union even beat America to space—putting the world's first satellite, Sputnik I, in earth's orbit as early as 1957. The evolution and development were so impressive, in fact, that even the White House's National Security Council looked on in awe. At one point, it described the threat posed by the Soviets as their 'proven ability to carry backward countries speedily through the crisis of modernization and industrialization'.[16]

But for all its impressive, eye-catching achievements, the Soviet communist model had one fatal flaw: it was not sustainable. The Soviet answer to any challenge was to throw *all* its resources at the problem forcibly, even if that was not efficient. It was like the Mughal larger-than-life style of development. Take the Taj Mahal, for instance. The Taj is an extraordinarily beautiful monument, but its construction did not involve path-breaking technological innovation or mechanical efficiency. Instead, the emperor pressed about 20,000 labourers and 1000 elephants to work on it for as long as twenty years. In the end, the Soviets did the same thing. They simply pressed their resources with little care for productivity or innovation. According to one estimate, the Soviet worker produced only about 38 per cent what an American produced per year.[17] And like the Mughals, the Soviets succeeded at grandiose missions that captured global attention, but they could not build an economy that was at the cutting edge.

Across the border, in China, Deng Xiaoping watched the Soviet economy unravel, starting from the mid-1970s. By 1989, the Soviet Union's story was finished—and the world's most successful communist experiment was over. So, a decade earlier, Deng had begun setting China off on its own path of development—more in line with the mores of globalization and economic openness. As one Chinese joke goes, Deng signalled a left turn and then went right.

Today, China's economic model is hardly that of a liberal capitalist economy, but it is certainly anything but communism. The Chinese Dream—as Xi now calls it—is a unique narrative. Its economy is dominated by state-owned enterprises (while three-fourths of India's GDP is estimated to come from the private sector). Its politics is monopolized by one party. But its one-party system works better than that of other countries, because it is set upon a ruthlessly professional bureaucracy which functions more on merit than those of other one-party states. Like India, China has had the historic advantage of a mature civil service, which has functioned across time and knows its job well. The machine, therefore, runs on its own.

The Chinese model naturally has its charms for the developing world. Unlike America, China started off from a low base, suffering from many of the same crippling challenges that much of the developing world still faces. Unlike Singapore, China's transformation took place on a humongous scale—in the world's most populous country. Under Mao, China had been to hell and back; his Great Leap Forward caused deadly famines and his Cultural Revolution sparked off widespread violence. If the Chinese model could take a massive country out of all of that and lift several millions out of poverty, it is inevitable that Tanzanians and Tunisians would find it appealing. And so they do: In the 2014 Afrobarometer survey held across Africa, China emerged as the second most appealing development model, and in Central Africa, it was even overwhelmingly voted as the best.[18]

Over the years, Beijing has sought to ride this wave—particularly in Africa, the world's newest workshop for state-building and geopolitical influence. The earliest port of entry for the Chinese Dream on the continent was Ethiopia—one of Africa's great symbols of freedom and pan-Africanism. In 1991, the left-leaning Ethiopian People's Revolutionary Democratic Front (EPRDF) came to power in Addis Ababa and soon began courting Beijing. Three years into office, the EPRDF sent a delegation to Beijing in order to seek 'China's advice on Ethiopia's development'.

Then, in 2005, there came a significant turning point. Ethiopia held a relatively free, fair and open election that year—and it resulted in a poor result for the EPRDF. Opposition groups, who had since then sat on the margins of Ethiopian politics, captured a third of the seats in Parliament. The EPRDF responded with a crackdown. Some opposition groups subsequently boycotted the government, others fled the country, and still others ended up in jail.

The EPRDF began looking east to Beijing, and Beijing responded. The Chinese helped the EPRDF set up a central party school on the lines of the Chinese Communist Party's own school in Beijing. It also designed a party cadre education system for the EPRDF, teaching them how to manage their own organizational structure, build an ideology, develop a propaganda system and so on. Senior Ethiopian training delegations regularly visited Beijing for further education, each time focusing on a different theme—from poverty alleviation to youth development.[19] The mentorship worked. For nearly three decades, the EPRDF ruled in Addis Ababa as a virtual one-party state, winning elections comfortably each time (until it was dissolved in 2019). The former prime minister, Meles Zenawi, often played the role of Beijing's spokesperson in Africa. He once said, 'Africa will never forget the historical role played by China in the struggle against colonialism.' On Chinese leadership in Africa, he said, 'Good governance can only come from inside; it cannot be imposed from outside. That was always an illusion. What the Chinese have done is explode that illusion.'

The Chinese communist party has used its fabled strength and effectiveness to great advantage elsewhere too. In South Africa, it has given similar mentorship to multiple political parties—from the South African Communist Party (SACP) to even the ruling African National Congress (ANC). In 2016, the SACP general secretary, Blade Nzimande, led a delegation to China to study socialism theories and practices. Zimbabwe's omnipotent Zimbabwe African National Union–Patriotic Front (ZANU-PF)—the party of Robert Mugabe—is another famous mentee of the Chinese.

China has tended to keep its political influence activities low-profile. Beijing is extremely sensitive to the optics of 'interfering in another sovereign state' (even if it does interfere when it wants to—as in Sudan or Zimbabwe). That has led many to say that China no longer has any interest in spreading communism the way Mao had done. That is fair and accurate—China does not want to spread *communism* around the world. But it certainly does want to leverage its one-party bureaucratic state model for

political influence overseas. And that is a sensible pursuit, from
Beijing's viewpoint.

Restoring the Laws of the Wild

What does all this mean for the Chinese world order? Like India,
China was one of the big gainers of globalization through the
1990s and the 2000s. In a country where consumers don't spend
quite as heavily, the Chinese Dream has been heavily dependent
on the sale of Chinese exports. That is why, in 2001, China
joined the World Trade Organization, against all its deeply held
ideological convictions. And ever since, Beijing has been quite
unequivocal in calling for stronger economic links across the
world and trade liberalization.

But unlike in India and the US—where the private sector plays a
big role—Chinese economic growth, trade and foreign investment
are much more heavily state-dominated. This has significant
implications for how Beijing approaches the more political aspects
of international cooperation. As we will see in chapter 5, India
and the US have significant interests in maintaining a certain set
of norms in policymaking worldwide (including towards rule of
law, ease of business, property rights, transparency in policymaking
and so on). These norms create favourable political and economic
conditions for private firms to trade and invest across borders.

But China has no use for such norms. As David Dollar pointed
out, Chinese investment is content with basic political stability, even
if a country's state institutions lack transparency and rule of law. The
key reason for this is that Chinese investment is driven by the state.
So long as there is a reliable and stable government in place, Beijing
will sign a government-to-government deal to create favourable
policies for all its investment projects, regardless of how that
country's state institutions and laws function with respect to other
firms. For instance, when its state-owned investments are threatened,

the Chinese government can simply hold the government in that country accountable under their deal. (By contrast, when an Indian or American firm finds its interests threatened, it would need to rely on the local courts and rule of law in that country.) Further, because Chinese investment is state-driven, its objectives are not purely economic; they are also political and strategic. Indian and American firms cannot go to treacherous parts of the world to cop business losses, but Chinese firms can—*provided* that such investment creates political and strategic benefits for Beijing.

On the other hand, international laws and norms are a menace for Beijing. China does not like being told what to do. It will not agree to norms regarding property rights, human rights, intellectual rights—or any rights—unless the Party believes that they will strengthen its own political standing (typically, they will not). In the 1990s, Beijing agreed to sign up to various international institutions, not because it agreed with their norms but because that was the only way to bring in investment. But Xi is right to believe that China is now large and strong enough to throw off the shackles and still survive.

And in recent times, international laws and institutions have increasingly come at odds with Chinese interests. China threw out the international tribunal ruling on the South China Sea in 2016 and it opened the Asian Investment Infrastructure Bank, in large part because it dislikes the World Bank's norms on human rights and the environment.* But there have also been other irritants for Beijing: As the COVID-19 pandemic raged in 2020, reports began to surface, indicating that Chinese authorities had covered up the earliest cases from public attention. Medical professionals who sought to raise the alarm as early as in December 2019 were either suppressed or jailed (one of the leading whistle-blowers, Li Wenliang, ultimately died of the disease).

---

* More on this in chapter 5.

But as it turned out, there was space for recourse under international law: After the Chinese government had similarly covered up early cases of the SARS (Severe Acute Respiratory Syndrome) epidemic in the early 2000s, the World Health Organization (WHO) adopted new international norms which required countries to 'report all events that could result in public health emergencies of international concern'. As reports of China's early cover-ups came to light, analysts urged the international community to consider remedies under the law, including removal of China from positions of membership. And the crisis induced a strong propaganda response from Beijing to undo the damage.

International law is generally toothless in terms of recourse after wrongdoing. China is unlikely to suffer for its disregard for international norms. But think about what might have happened if China was a democracy: Independent state institutions would have detected the epidemic early and the president would not have been able to stop them from raising the alarm. In the event that a cover-up was still successful, it would have brought about an inevitable change in government as the virus took lives—which in itself would have been 'recourse' for the rest of the world. Instead, the opposite happened. As one commentator pointed out in the *War on the Rocks* blog, 'Chinese tycoon Ren Zhiqiang lambasted Xi for his mishandling of the coronavirus, calling him a "power-hungry clown". Ren soon disappeared.'[20]

Nonetheless, Beijing is unlikely to want to sustain or promote norms and laws on the world stage which would curtail its own sovereign actions. In recent years, China has been expanding its influence at various UN agencies to try and work around international norms and institutions. Beijing is now the second-largest contributor to the UN budget—accounting for 12 per cent of its funding as opposed to just 1 per cent two decades ago. It is also now the only country in UN history to feature among both the top financiers as well as the top troop contributors of UN peacekeeping. More importantly, it is forging strong alliances with other developing countries and supporting the candidature of their officials to top UN posts—leaving these agencies with friendly and pliable functionaries.

The influence seems to be paying off. In the early 2000s, under the leadership of the Norwegian doctor Gro Harlem Brundtland, the WHO had taken Beijing to task for its SARS cover-ups and even made history by announcing a travel ban in and out of southern China to control the epidemic. But in 2020, the WHO—under a different chief, Ethiopia's Tedros Adhanom Ghebreyesus—has toed much closer to China's rhetoric. In mid-January, it echoed China's false claim that the coronavirus does not transmit from human to human. Tedros also criticized countries early on for applying travel restrictions out of China, before inevitably advocating lockdowns and social distancing. What changed between the early 2000s and 2020? China's influence did. Tedros is a product of Ethiopia's EPRDF. He was also elected the WHO chief under China's patronage.

Beijing wants to retain the right to put the Party's interests above popular interests. In recent years, Russia and China have together combined—owing to commonalities in their domestic politics—to launch a rebellion against international institutions and to instate the 'might is right' policy in international law. They aren't doing that by throwing out international institutions; instead, they are collaborating to increase their footprint and change how international institutions work.

DND: Democracy Next Door

If the Chinese Dream is to be successfully exported to the world stage, it must first continue to flourish in China. In recent times, that has gotten increasingly difficult. When he first unveiled his conception of the Chinese Dream, President Xi Jinping was quite clear that it was a dream for the collective, not the individual. Only when the country is doing well, he said, the people can prosper. Individual rights are allowed, but only in the pursuit of innovation to strengthen the national economy—and thereby help further accumulate wealth and power (think fuqiang).[21]

In recent years, Xi has made clear that—to him—the Chinese Dream precludes any democratic aspirations that may challenge his power. Instead, the president has offered the Chinese a personality cult rivalling that of Mao himself. In 2018, Xi did away with term limits for the president, effectively opening up a path for him to become the Chinese Vladimir Putin.

The Internet has often countered all this with comic relief, and when it has, Beijing has responded through censoring—a phenomenon now widely infamous as the 'Great Firewall of China'. In 2013, memes began surfacing on social media, comparing the rotund, smiling president to Winnie the Pooh. In response, the Chinese government banned all references to 'Pooh' on the Internet. Since then, the slope has been slippery: By mid-2013, the government had begun banning random words which were seen as a threat to the president's authority. These included 'today', 'tomorrow' and even the humble 'toad'.[22]

In traditional problem areas, such as Tibet, Xinjiang, Hong Kong and Taiwan, Xi's crackdown has not been so funny.

In these areas, the problem—put simply—is cultural diversity. Chinese political culture and centralization—all of which led to the entrenchment of the Confucian ideals of order and stability— were much more dominant in areas where the Han have lived for centuries, free from foreign influence. The remote western parts of China, which have long been difficult to access from where the Chinese state has always ruled, have been much more 'vulnerable' to foreign influence: The Turks, the Arabs and the Central Asians often brought their cultural, social and political practices here. In Hong Kong, ties with the British led to stronger cultural globalization, along with economic and political openness. The result has been that, over the years, the Uighurs, Tibetans and Hong Kongers have built their own identities, cut off from the Han majority. Their allegiance to mainstream Chinese identity, which is decidedly monoethnic and monocultural, is hence much weaker.

In response to these challenges, Xi has launched iron-fisted efforts to spread and uphold the dominant Chinese political culture and social order. In Xinjiang, the government began all but banning the very practice of Islam, including fasts during Ramadan and even a ridiculous ban on the name 'Muhammad'. But since 2017, Beijing has gone much further—that was the year when it started putting over a million Uighur Muslims in what were essentially concentration camps (Beijing called these 're-education camps'—a fancy word for the indoctrination of the Uighurs in the worship of the Communist Party). In the autonomous territory of Hong Kong, Xi's constant efforts to meddle in democratic elections—including by deciding who runs and who wins—seem to have met the end of the citizenry's patience. As of late 2020, Hong Kong has been paralysed by months of protests—sometimes even violent ones—directed at seeking independence from mainland China.

On the other hand, the Han-dominated heartland of China has generally remained loyal to the Party for decades. Deng's reforms created both wealth and power, which strengthened the legitimacy of the Party's rule in the eyes of many Han Chinese. But even that could now be in peril: With wealth having been created, the Chinese have had their basic needs satisfied. They may soon start seeking other needs—including the aspiration for political freedom. There are already signs of discontent. According to a 2015 report from Human Rights Watch, China sees an estimated 1,00,000 'mass protests' each year—with a hundred people or more.[23] Beijing is also wary of commemorations of the 1989 Tiananmen protests and pre-emptively jails hundreds of activists each June, ahead of its anniversary.

Xi has tried to counter these problems by predictably drilling in the importance of 'order and stability' for China's sustained growth. He has also repeatedly emphasized the perils of a chaotic democracy in its place. The state-run Xinhua news network publishes multiple commentary pieces each year with the same theme: Western democracy does not work, and 'Chinese democracy' has created wealth. The articles often use the same phrases and words over and over each year: In two articles published in March 2018 and then March 2019, Xinhua uses the phrase, 'Democracy is not a decoration, but a means of solving problems.' (Funnily enough, the two articles were supposedly written or edited by two different people.) In March 2019, Xinhua declared, 'Chinese democracy puts Western illusion in dust.'

An especially special place is reserved for Indian democracy. In a revealing essay for the *World Policy Journal* in 2013, journalist Li Xin wrote, 'In official discourse, China's largest neighbour is often cited as a prime example of why democracy doesn't work. India, known as the world's largest democracy, is deemed dysfunctional.' Among several other examples, Li Xin quotes a paper published by the Central Party School, the Communist Party's training academy and an influential organ of state propaganda. Its authors wrote, 'While democracy is widely expected to control corruption, by commonly used yardsticks, democratic India has done no better than China at checking corruption, and may even have fared worse.'[24]

Some Chinese dissidents have even looked to New Delhi for support. Everybody knows about the most famous of these cases: The Tibetan government-in-exile headed by the Dalai Lama has been hosted in India for over fifty years. But even in more recent times, democracy activists in China have been hopeful of Indian patronage and support. In 2016, prominent dissident leaders from China planned a conference in India to discuss the prospects for democracy in their country. New Delhi even facilitated the conference at first, granting visas to the attendants. But in a curious

U-turn, conspicuously following Beijing's dismay over the event, the Indian government subsequently revoked the visas.[25]

The threat of a successful and stable democracy next door is very real for the Communist Party. But India would be an even bigger threat to the Party if New Delhi managed to beat Beijing at the game of fuqiang—wealth and power. Communist Party propaganda has long depended on the argument that its one-party rule 'Chinese democracy' has been successful in creating wealth and power for the Chinese. But if India were to ever match up to the Chinese, the Party's legitimacy would be under serious threat. This is a threat which, in many ways, is much stronger than the threat of American democracy. America's success is easily explained away: It had a head start of some 200 years over the Chinese and began from a higher wealth base. It is also one-fourth of China's population. But on all these parameters, India is comparable to China—on population, on size and complexity, and even on the starting point: India and China were roughly just as rich at the start of the 1990s. And what's more—India was looted clean by two centuries of colonialism.

Dealing with the Dragon

The race is certainly well in China's favour; India is nowhere near as wealthy or prosperous as China. But Beijing does not typically believe in taking chances. In addition to its anti-democracy propaganda, China often takes steps to contain and put down New Delhi. These include the odd skirmish along the Himalayas, diplomatic prodding such as through the development of the infamous highway through Pakistan-controlled Kashmir, and even the periodic reminder that China holds a prestigious veto seat in the United Nations Security Council. It also means containing Indian influence—primarily in South Asia, where Beijing practises strategic encirclement à la wei qi.

China does not seek to destroy or maim India through a violent war like the Soviets and Americans had threatened to do. But it does see value in playing a game of wei qi to strategically contain it.

What should India do about all this?

Much like the conflict with Pakistan, Chinese activities in the Himalayas and across South Asia serve to keep India tangled up in South Asia. Beijing diverts New Delhi's focus and attention away from foreign policy opportunities in other parts of the world—even as China itself goes global. That is why China and India repeatedly find themselves stuck in recurring border standoffs every other year: from a standoff in Ladakh in 2014, to the Doklam standoff in Bhutan in 2017, to yet another standoff in Ladakh in 2020. And in the years ahead, it's well worth putting money on the possibility that the Chinese will keep coming and going, in and out of Indian-claimed territory in the Himalayas.

Chinese aggression in the Himalayas has a particularly profound effect on the psychology of Indian strategic thinking. It exploits the bitter memories of the 1962 war, which—to many people—was a sign that India was too weak to aspire for global leadership. It also stokes paranoia in New Delhi, particularly towards Nepal and Bhutan, which share borders with both India and China. In May 2020, as India and Nepal quibbled over a roadway on their disputed border, the Indian army chief insinuated that Kathmandu was being influenced by the Chinese. That comment was received just as well as one would expect, with many Nepalese commentators complaining that their sovereignty had been insulted. In 2017, the Doklam standoff similarly sullied India's relations with Bhutan.

India has only one credible way to deter Chinese aggression: to become a global power. India has to assume a more global role of its own—and build bargaining chips all over the world.[*] If India can gain influence and win over allies around the world, it would

_____

[*] How can India do this? More on that in chapter 6.

make itself significant and powerful enough to threaten Chinese aspirations and interests. In Asia and Africa, debt traps induced by BRI are gradually stoking discontent. In the South China Sea, China's neighbours are seeking support in standing up to Beijing. All of these provide India opportunities to insert itself as a counter-balancing force against China.

As Sun Tzu said, it is not wise to wage a war before you have won the war. Therefore, the best way to *prevent* a war with the Chinese is to make Beijing believe that it will not win.

5

The Old Guard

The World That America Built

No rising power excites America as much as India does. The think tanks and foreign policy circles of Washington and New York are filled with optimists—some of whom are more eager for India to become a global power than India is itself. Since the turn of the millennium, America has invested heavily in goading India to rise. Apart from eagerly advertising India's democratic credentials and multicultural society, American leaders have done other unusual things.

Take the nuclear issue—the most famous example of them all. Nuclear proliferation is a cause on which American foreign policy hawks have often justified war. Whatever the real impetus behind the invasion of Iraq, it was the supposed presence of nuclear weapons that had ignited the fury of the American public and created support for war. With Iran too, the threat of nuclear proliferation is the sole cause for a long-running feud between hardliners on both sides. Decades earlier, the presence of Soviet nuclear missiles in Cuba had driven one of the most serious crises in American foreign policy history.

Yet, with India, things have been different. While America levied sanctions on India for its nuclear tests, the crisis never reached the drastic enmity of Iran, Iraq or Cuba. And since the early 2000s, Washington has even *validated* India's status as a nuclear power—pushing for extraordinary exceptions under international law. The Bush administration used its political influence to allow India to deal and trade in nuclear technology without non-proliferation commitments. (Think about this: America has not even openly endorsed nuclear power status for *Israel* in this manner—a country that has arguably the most powerful lobby of support in Washington. When one thinks of Prime Minister Manmohan Singh's term in office, this achievement should get its fair due.)

America has also been among the most consistent and vocal advocates for a permanent India seat in the UN Security Council (alongside, perhaps, France). And that support has been bipartisan, running from Bush to Obama to Donald Trump. This is a more extraordinary phenomenon than most Indians realize: Since as long as history can remember, America has not invested like this in another country's prospects to be a dominant political power.

But the sponsorship has taken a long time coming—and the journey has not been easy. When India became independent in 1947, America saw a potential ally in the new republic. India proclaimed itself a multicultural democracy, saw unity in diversity, and committed to fundamental human rights and pluralism. More importantly, India was led by a Western-educated aristocrat in Nehru. Nehru knew the ways of the West, spoke fluent English and was therefore expected to be easily relatable.

Yet, Nehru's first visit to the United States saw him spar with American policymakers. Washington wanted India to be its ally in the Cold War against Soviet communism. But Nehru struggled to see a threat from the Soviets—he was himself an avowed practitioner of state planning and socialism, and saw these as being compatible with democracy. Washington also wanted India to subordinate itself to American foreign policy goals—as other American strategic allies did. But Nehru treasured independence in foreign policy and came from a school of Indian exceptionalism that found any subjugation of his civilization laughable.

The talks did not go well. In his memoirs later, the then Secretary of State, Dean Acheson, recalled his discussions with Nehru most painfully: '[He was] one of the most difficult men with whom I have ever had to deal,' Acheson wrote.[1] Acheson's successor, John Foster Dulles, proved to be even more combative. Exasperated by India's insistence on the pursuit of its own goals, he courted Pakistan instead. Pakistan and the United States signed a historically significant military pact in 1954 and set the foundations of a strategic alliance that lasted through the Cold War and beyond.

There were many key challenges and conflicts in the India–US relationship during the Cold War. The most insurmountable of them was, quite simply, a difference over what was important to each country. To America, it was the spread of communism. To India, it was the fight against colonial exploitation and racism. On every forum, Indian diplomats spoke about the exploitation of the poorer countries by the rich—through trade, military might and political influence. (To America, this was anathema.) India's postcolonial allies in Africa, Asia and Latin America also shared a deep scepticism for American power—and New Delhi invariably reflected that through the Non-Aligned Movement.

In the aftermath of the Cold War, as India opened its economy and society, things have changed. For its own growth and development, India has come to rely on globalization and the international institutions and norms which facilitate it—all of which were built by America due to similar economic interests of its own. Democracy and rule of law around the world are now important to both, in a way that it is not to China or Russia. All of this makes for a natural strategic alliance.

Yet, Americans are constantly frustrated with New Delhi. In Washington's ideal world, India would join America and its allies as one of the world's global policemen—and as a protector of human rights and democratic values worldwide. More pressingly, America would like India to uphold the international order that it has built: In the South China Sea, America would like India to take a more proactive interest in maintaining free navigation. In Afghanistan, America wants India to become a more proactive security partner. Everywhere in the world, America wants India to become a full member of the Western alliance, including commitments to act—whether militarily or otherwise—towards common purposes.

India is allergic to such alliances and commitments. Many of the old concerns that New Delhi had in the days of Nehru have not died—and it would take much more than just better chemistry between Indian and American leaders to change that. Some Indian strategists are not even sure if India should be as committed to America's world order. As one Indian diplomat told me at the UN, 'Let the Chinese build their world and we will still adapt to it.' But is that an approach which will satisfy India's interests? Or will it imperil India's rise? More intriguingly, why does America care about India stepping up to guard its world order in the era of the global Chinese Dream? And given how reluctant New Delhi seems, why doesn't America give up and cultivate other allies instead to take over as the new guard?

In God's Name We Trust

Through the 1800s, America followed an Indira Gandhi–style foreign policy: cynical, militaristic and neighbourhood-centric. The key proponent of that policy was President James Monroe, who served in office from 1817 to 1825. In 1823, Monroe introduced his doctrine for the first time during his State of the Union address to the US Congress. European colonialism was still running on full steam in other parts of the world at the time—and Monroe saw potential European influence west of the Atlantic as a direct threat to America's own primacy in its neighbourhood. So he declared that keeping Europe out of the Americas should be a key objective of US foreign policy. Monroe asked that Europe refrain from colonizing the newly independent countries in the Americas. In return, he said, America would continue to remain neutral on the affairs of existing European colonies.

The Monroe doctrine was an extension of America's long-standing policy of keeping to itself. As the Harvard historian Samuel Eliot Morison put it, 'As early as 1783 . . . the United States adopted the policy of isolation and announced its intention to keep out of Europe. The supplementary principle of the Monroe Doctrine [was] that Europe must keep out of America.'[2]

The Monroe Doctrine's isolationist approach remained a key tenet of US foreign policy all through the nineteenth century. It even withstood the first half of World War I: For two and a half years after the start of World War I, President Woodrow Wilson continued to assert that America had no business interfering in Europe's problems—and he strove hard to keep the US out of the war. But as it wore on, Wilson's commitment and patience were tested. In 1914, the American press splashed reports on Germany's occupation and atrocities in Belgium—infamously called the 'Rape of Belgium'. In 1915, Germany sank a British passenger liner via a submarine attack. By 1917, German aggression had reached America's own shores. Early that year, British intelligence officers intercepted a German telegram to Mexico, promising to help Mexico regain the territories it had lost to America during a war in the mid-1800s. Then, around the same time, German submarines began targeting American merchant ships in the Atlantic.

All this had poisoned American public opinion against Germany. Berlin was now seen as a 'threat to democracy' in America, Europe and everywhere else—and public concern began to bother the president. In April 1917, the anti-war Wilson told Congress that America had no choice but to enter the War against Germany. He reasoned that, despite his reluctance, Germany's aggression now endangered freedom and democracy around the world. 'The world must be made safe for democracy,' Wilson said. 'Its peace must be planted upon the tested foundations of political liberty.'[3]

America's entry into World War I was a watershed moment in world history. It marked—for the first time—a US foreign policy initiative, driven by public opinion, to fulfil interests that were far from the homeland. America was not quite threatened by German aggression as Western Europe was; the Atlantic made sure of that. A policy of isolation could easily have been sustained by a more inward-looking nation. If things got too bad, Wilson could have simply accepted Germany as the inevitable overlord of Europe— and signed a peace deal with them. But stories of oppression and atrocities across the ocean hammered away at the American public, which believed that it had to do something. As Wilson himself told Congress, 'We have no selfish ends to serve. We desire no conquest, no dominion . . . We are but one of the champions of the rights of mankind.'[4]

Democracy, in the colonial age, was a largely European phenomenon, and many Americans felt a deep connect with Western Europe (the UK and France, in particular). This was due both to cultural ties and the camaraderie for fellow democracies.

But there were other philosophical factors that were shaping the American public to be more outward-looking, activistic and humanitarian than publics in other parts of the world. For much of contemporary history, Americans have been more religious than the Europeans—a fact that holds to this day. But they also define American national pride and exceptionalism in very religious terms. A recurring theme in American politics and foreign policy discourse is the idea that the United States is God's 'chosen nation' with the mandate to uphold freedom in the world. This is an idea with bipartisan support, which has survived through the ages. Abraham Lincoln once said America is 'the last, best hope of earth'. A century later, Richard Nixon said, 'America came into the world 180 years ago not just to have freedom for ourselves, but to carry it to the whole world.' During World War II, Franklin D. Roosevelt told Congress: 'We on our side are striving to be true to [our] divine heritage.'[5]

The idea that America is God's 'chosen nation' has been used and misused by various presidents over the years. Politicians often use political ideologies to justify actions that are driven by other underlying motives. The most infamous of these was George W. Bush, who sought to defend his militaristic foreign policy in the Middle East by beckoning America's divine mandate to 'help the spread of freedom' around the world. Yet, the notable fact is that this philosophy appeals to the American public, in ways that it would not in other countries: Many Americans *genuinely believe* in their divine mandate and advocate an activist foreign policy. When the *New York Times* writes stories about a drowning Syrian toddler in the Mediterranean Sea, it has an impact on public opinion, which nudges foreign policy in a certain direction. When CNN airs pictures of Rohingyas floating in small boats in the Bay of Bengal, it has the same impact of awakening the American activist's conscience. As one snarky French diplomat joked to me at the UN, 'The UN Security Council has six permanent members: America, France, Britain, Russia, China—and CNN.'

The humanitarianism of the American public suffered most during the Cold War—and it has had lasting consequences for America's credibility in the postcolonial world. During the Cold War, the fight against communism justified all ends and all means. Around the world, America backed autocratic despots against democratically elected leaders, if the latter were inclined to follow socialist policies. In Chile, the role of the CIA in helping the notorious dictator Augusto Pinochet come to power still riles up the local people. In the Philippines, America backed another notorious autocrat, Ferdinand Marcos, because it was spooked by the communist alternatives to him. Even Saddam Hussein was at one point an American pawn in the fight against communism. As Dulles is supposed to have once said of anti-communist dictators, 'If he is a bas---d, at least he is our bas---d.'[6]

But the realpolitik of the Cold War stemmed less from a dilution of the humanitarian activism of the American public and more from a misguided prioritisation of the fear of communism. If the American public had not been so strongly convinced by their politicians of the 'terror of communism', negative public opinion towards Pinochet and others may have had consequences for US foreign policy. Under Ronald Reagan, America backed a popular democratic uprising against Marcos in the Philippines. Journalists and activists at the time argued that Reagan simply had to back the Filipino rebellion—it held little threat of a communist revolution.

Why America Built the World

Wars are costly, except when they aren't. The fragility of post-war Europe—and the beginning of the end of European colonialism—had been most fortuitous for two new global powers. In the aftermath of World War II, Europe's self-destruction left the United States as the world's foremost power. Americans were responsible for a whopping 45 per cent of the world's economic production, and the first successful use of nuclear weapons had made the US an intimidating military power. But on the other side of Europe, there was the Soviet Union—another humongous country which had brushed aside the costs of the war and was launching itself on its own mission for global power.

The Soviets provided the world's first real experiment of communism—and they offered it as an alternative to America's capitalist democracy. In many parts of the postcolonial world, people were still reeling from their humiliating exploitation by the rich and powerful; communism seemed to them a more poverty-friendly model to adopt. As European occupation was retreating, postcolonial leaders flocked to Moscow for patronage and support.

To fight back, Washington began building a web of international institutions to promote its *own* norms and principles for economic growth. In 1944, the US brought together forty-four countries at the town of Bretton Woods in New Hampshire to discuss the reconstruction of the post-war world and work towards the end of economic protectionism. After a conference lasting three weeks, a final agreement was drawn up to create two key institutions that would fulfil those ends: the International Bank of Reconstruction and Development (IBRD) and the International Monetary Fund.* While the IBRD was aimed at lending money for infrastructure projects in countries ravaged by the war, the IMF's core objective was to maintain stability in the global economy, by promoting linkages and financial flows across nations. The general idea behind the two institutions was to promote capitalist ideals, economic openness and market liberalization.

The Soviets attended the Bretton Woods conference and signed its final agreement. But they later refused to ratify it. They also chose not to attend the inauguration of the IBRD and the IMF, and never joined the two institutions for the entirety of their existence.

As the American economy globalized and developed linkages with the rest of the world (starting with its own Western European allies), Washington built other institutions to coordinate—and regulate—policymaking around the world. To transact internationally, American businesses needed a favourable

---

* The IBRD is a component of the World Bank, which comprises of the IBRD and the International Development Association (IDA). The IDA is primarily responsible for giving concessional loans to the poorest countries. The IMF—on the other hand—is not part of the World Bank.

investment climate in various countries. This included state institutions that uphold transparency in rule-making, maintain rule of law, and protect the rights of businesses and investors. So Washington established bodies that laid down standards and norms for everything, from intellectual property rights, to air transport safety, vaccination and, of course, trade. Most of these were brought under the umbrella of the United Nations—an organization itself propelled by an American president, headquartered in New York, and most heavily funded by the United States. Treaties were signed to hold countries accountable to these norms.

Then came the need for stability and security worldwide—the issue on which American intervention draws the most flak around the world. Here, too, there were economic interests at play, in addition to national security concerns. By the mid-1960s, Americans were already investing more than $1.5 billion abroad—steadily growing with each passing year. Fragile states were increasingly posing a threat to the survival of these investments abroad. This incentivized intervention from Washington in problem areas of the world—particularly in developing economies.

As American businesses grew, they also became increasingly dependent on foreign resources—from labour to oil to consumer markets. Oil crises such as the one in the 1970s—which were often closely related to the intractable conflict between Israel and the Arabs—brought the US to the Middle East. Each time there was any displeasure in the region, the Arab oil exporters would voluntarily (or involuntarily) boost oil prices through supply shortages. For Washington, this was a problem—so it cultivated close ties with whichever politician it considered to be most likely to uphold stability in the region.

To keep unfavourable leaders (sponsored by the Soviets) out of power in different parts of the world, America extended its security cover, building numerous alliance blocs such as the North Atlantic Treaty Organization (NATO) in Europe and the

South East Asia Treaty Organization (SEATO) in South East Asia, and developing military bases on almost every continent. Indeed, even this objective of keeping the Soviets out was often driven by economic interests: A Soviet-sponsored communist leader would have introduced protectionist policies which would have hurt American investment, trade and business interests.

In the post–Cold War world, America has continued to use this security cover to maintain its global influence. In some places, it has extended its nuclear umbrella to support allies—and deter them from developing their own nuclear weapons (Saudi Arabia, Japan and South Korea, for instance).

So far as possible, Washington also had an incentive to act in accordance with international law on matters such as trade and international security, as opposed to working unilaterally. This was because American security and economic interests needed *other countries* to also abide by the norms and laws of these international institutions. Therefore, while it used its clout to influence the norms and laws drawn up by international institutions, the US also abided by them and worked to strengthen them. (Whenever Washington flouts international institutions—such as during the invasion of Iraq—it has, in fact, lost its political capital quite heavily and alienated its own allies.)

This reliance on a web of multilateral institutions to support its own interests—also known as 'stakeholder hegemony'—had several other unintended benefits for US foreign policy influence. It made American power more palatable to other countries by binding its foreign policy actions to mutually agreed international law—and reduced Washington's ability to act arbitrarily on the world stage. In 1965, Secretary of State Dean Rusk told the US Senate Foreign Relations Committee of the expanding scale of these commitments: 'We are every day, in one sense, accepting limitations upon our complete freedom of action,' he said. 'We have more than 4300 treaties and international agreements, two-thirds of which have been entered into in the past twenty-five years . . . each one of which at least limits our freedom of action.'[7]

International institutions somewhat curbed arbitrary US actions, streamlined and coordinated policymaking around the world in pursuit of globalization (a key US economic interest), and minimized pushback to American hegemony. They also exported the principles of American policymaking to the rest of the world by turning them into international standards and norms for governance. In many ways, they were a good use of American national power. But they also formed the foundations of American influence around the world. It was a good bargain for the world's superpower.

United States of America 2.0?

India has a unique identity crisis. It is an instinctively Western country in Eastern clothes.

As prime minister, Jawaharlal Nehru often pushed the idea that he was a representative of a resurgent Asia. As early as March 1947, New Delhi hosted an Asian Relations Conference, bringing together twenty-eight countries, spanning from Arabia to Korea. Nehru delivered a characteristically eloquent inaugural address with Mahatma Gandhi in the audience. Asia had suddenly become important in world affairs, he said, and its countries could no longer be used as pawns by others: 'The old imperialisms are fading away' and leaving a resurgent new Asia in their wake.[8] In the years that followed, Nehru began his role as spokesperson for the postcolonial world by courting Asia. Unlike the West, Nehru said, Asia had thousands of years of civilizational experience and knowledge behind it—all of which could no longer be subdued or shackled in the new world order.

These were ideas filled with political romance, and they certainly appealed to Asians for a while. But in truth, neither the prime minister nor his newly independent republic was authentically

Asian. Many of India's stalwarts—and, in particular, those who laid the foundations of the republic—were educated in the West: Nehru and Gandhi in Britain, and Ambedkar in the United States. The legal framework they laid down for the new country was therefore naturally influenced by Western liberal thought. India's democratic state institutions resembled Western Europe and North America more than they did East Asia or the Middle East.

Over time, these early trends have only further exacerbated themselves. In the age of globalization, few Eastern societies have opened themselves to Western cultural influences as liberally as India has. India is today one of the world's largest English-speaking nations, with nearly as many Indians speaking the language as the entire population of the United States. Western movies, shows, books, music and cuisine are becoming increasingly popular—even in rural areas, aided by the Internet. The cultural influence runs both ways: Indian cultural exports—films, music and literature— are often more easily relatable to fellow democratic societies in the West than exports from other parts of Asia.

Even economically—as we saw in chapter 2—India has come to be bizarrely structured. India is more reliant on its services sector than most countries in its income group or at its level of development. While most developing economies focus on agriculture and manufacturing to create growth, India's growth story has looked more West-like. Like in America's economy, well over half of India's GDP is projected to come from the services sector in the years ahead—including high-skilled areas such as IT (the most famous Indian export), finance and banking. The services sector is also expanding its share of the exports pie: According to government data, India's services export between April and July in 2019 grew by 8.65 per cent relative to the same period the previous year. By contrast, exports in goods contracted by 0.37 per cent. While agriculture still employs the majority of the Indian labour force, that is also naturally changing: Farmers now aspire to educate their children, so as to take advantage of the high-growth, high-skilled sector.

The future also looks decidedly more Western than Asian: Many Indians fixate on the manufacturing sector as the panacea of India's poverty ills. This is the traditional model of growth—to go from an agrarian economy to a manufacturing power to, finally, a services-dominated workforce. But as we have seen in chapter 2, India's natural trajectory seems decidedly reliant on the modern services sector. The aspirations of the rural farming folk are also more towards higher-paying skilled services jobs, rather than factory work.

But there is a more important and consequential similarity: In the post-liberalization era, India's economy has become more reliant on the private sector for growth and investment—both Indian companies as well as foreign ones. As we saw in chapter 2, the mixture of globalization, English-speaking skills and high-skill technical education has, over time, created a fairly professional and mature Indian private corporate sector—sometimes rivalling the West in its organizational capacity and well ahead of the private sector in any comparable developing economy. India's private sector now increasingly harbours more aggressive aspirations for foreign expansion and investment: In the three years between April 2017 and April 2020, Indians invested over $43 million overseas—up by almost a third from the preceding three years.[9] In recent years, Indian automobile companies such as TVS have opened manufacturing factories in South East Asia to create tailormade products for that developing market.

All these striking similarities have created several unforeseen foreign policy interests for India that resemble those of the US. Like the Americans, Indian workers and businesses in foreign countries need a local government which protects their private investments, human rights and property through effective rule of law. They also need competitive, open markets which would allow the many private Indian firms to thrive, rather than closed economies which propagate monopolies. (But contrast all this to the nature of Chinese economic interests from chapter 4.)

For all these reasons, Indians stand to gain from the norms and policies promoted by international institutions and agencies. On energy, India's heavy dependence on oil imports harks back to the American economy in the twentieth century—which makes peace and stability in the Middle East especially important.

Indian state institutions are also more Western in nature, making American norms more relevant. Free trade and immigration—issues which Washington championed very strongly, except under the Trump administration—are essential for the core of India's development. And then, of course, there is the more general affinity for democracy itself—whose presence in the world increases India's soft power, economic gains and foreign policy influence considerably, as it did with the United States.

As a developing economy, India still takes some policy stances which stand somewhat contrary to the norms of America's international institutions: On the issue of intellectual property rights, for instance, India is still quite inimical to Washington. But these are policy stances which owe more to domestic political currents than to long-term economic interest—Indian politics is still inherently protectionist, although globalization, trade and openness have for long been the key drivers of its growth. And in recent years, public opinion has been seen to change rapidly against such protectionism. While a closed economy was once celebrated in India, elections are today increasingly driven by promises of economic reform and liberalization. The service of successive Western-educated liberal economists at the central bank and on economic policy councils has also stood testament to that trend.

It is no wonder then that New Delhi has become somewhat of a free-rider on American power. Indian diplomats would not typically say that their national interests are fulfilled by the norms and institutions built by the US—or by Washington's foreign policy influence. (Such talk runs counter to the 'strategic independence' that they hold dear.) But the truth is that India has benefited enormously across sectors from American presence or influence. Take Afghanistan. Over the years, that country has become a major project of state-building for New Delhi. Apart from training and equipment for security forces, India has also spent close to $1 billion (and possibly more) building schools, hospitals and other infrastructure in war-torn areas. India also invested heavily in building Afghan democratic institutions: It provided funds to develop a robust media sector, built the Parliament building, and helped develop an election process.

When Washington first indicated that it would withdraw its forces from Afghanistan, New Delhi was among the most nervous. With militants infesting large swathes of the country and no boots of its own on the ground, India had come to rely on America's security cover for its many activities. Washington too liked the norms and institutions that New Delhi was exporting to Afghanistan. (Similarly, New Delhi has been quietly benefited by US presence in the South China Sea and the Indian Ocean— free navigation and trade flows being common concerns for both countries.)

India has also benefited from US-led international institutions. Apart from the economic reasons, there are many compelling political reasons as well: Given that New Delhi has limited military presence or coercive power around the world, the podiums and frameworks of international institutions have been crucial for the pursuit of its interests. Nehru used the UN to great effect in burnishing his status as a postcolonial representative, and over the years, India's biggest role and impact on international security has come through participation in UN peacekeeping. On the economic front, it was the IMF that came to the rescue when India's economy was at risk of collapse in the early 1990s. In more recent years, treaties and provisions under the World Trade Organization have helped New Delhi benefit from free and fair trade—and also pursue redressal under WTO norms when its interests have been threatened.* There are also other easily neglected benefits: International institutions have become fairly significant employers of Indian talent, especially owing to their multilingual skills and proficiency in English.

As India grows into a global power, its incentives to help continue the American world order—to partner with Washington in the duty of its maintenance—will only increase. And Washington is acutely aware of that convergence in interests—as is China.

Buying a Seat at the Table

The Soviets never joined the World Bank or the IMF, but China did—and Beijing is today the second-most influential member of the World Bank by voting power. Yet, like the Soviets before them, China has long been disgusted with the liberal economics and pro-democracy tendencies of the World Bank and the IMF. The two Bretton Woods institutions routinely attach strings and conditions to their loans and financial assistance—ranging from political considerations such as the guarantee of human rights, to economic ones such as tight government budgets and market liberalization. To Beijing, all of these are anathema to its natural political character.

In 2015, therefore, China launched its own rebel organization, the Asian Infrastructure Investment Bank. With the AIIB, Beijing wanted to make a political statement: to give loans to developing countries with no strings attached and few questions asked. In

---

* Ironically, this had been particularly important in the Trump era. India had successfully challenged certain Trump administration tariffs at the WTO.

Article 31, the AIIB's Articles of Agreement say, 'The Bank, its President, officers and staff shall not interfere in the political affairs of any member, nor shall they be influenced in their decisions by the political character of the member concerned.'[10]

The US almost immediately saw the AIIB as a threat to its world order and hegemony. But to Washington's chagrin, India joined the Chinese as a founding member—and became the AIIB's second-most important member state. In the months that followed, Washington took great pains to prevent other allies from joining the AIIB. Yet, every other day, one of them flocked away: Germany, Australia, South Korea and even the UK. Even *Japanese officials*—the most pro-American and Chinese-sceptic of them all—have publicly considered joining the bank.

In most cases, an American ally joined the AIIB in order to maintain strong economic ties with the Chinese—and to benefit from Beijing's investment spree. But in India's case, these were not strong determinants. New Delhi has been decidedly vocal against other Chinese initiatives—most importantly, BRI, the very source of Chinese investment. It also did not share China's distaste for the World Bank's ideological inclinations. While New Delhi does not mind a no-interference policy, it did not also mind the principles of the World Bank: Many of these are in line with India's own political convictions and its chosen path of economic development.

And the World Bank likes India too. Between 1945 and 2019, India was the highest recipient of World Bank assistance by a country mile, accounting for a whopping $115 billion. The second-largest recipient was China—at just over half that amount. More tellingly, just under half of India's borrowing came from the International Development Association (IDA)—the component of the World Bank which provides low-interest 'soft' loans for development. In all, India has accounted for more than 13 per cent of the assistance that the IDA has paid out since 1945, despite not being among the poorest countries for a fair few years now.[11]

The problem New Delhi had was not that the World Bank and the IMF are terrible; it was that it didn't have as much of a voice at the decision-making table as it wanted. Decision-making in both institutions is dominated by the West. Of the World Bank's fourteen presidents so far, thirteen have been American nationals (the exception was from Bulgaria). All of the IMF's managing directors so far have been Europeans. Despite some changes to the voting powers at the World Bank in recent years, India still lags behind France and the UK quite significantly—even though all three countries have comparable economic size. Not surprisingly, each year, New Delhi asks the World Bank to give it stronger voting powers at the bank.

But at the AIIB, New Delhi has got the red-carpet treatment. It is the second-most influential member state behind China—with more voting power than the likes of Germany, France and the UK. It has a seat on the powerful twelve-member board of directors. Indian representatives have also been given positions of high standing at the bank—including the post of the vice president and chief investment officer.

India's biggest grouse with America's network of international norms and institutions is not that they are all inherently wrong, but that it does not have a seat at the table. For close to two decades, New Delhi has been pushing to set this right—at various organs of the UN, the World Bank, the IMF and even bodies that regulate defence trade and technology.

In recent years, Washington has also responded. Apart from advocacy at the UN Security Council, it has also been an ardent voice of support for India's membership in the Nuclear Suppliers Group (NSG), which controls nuclear trade. In 2018, Washington publicly said that India meets all qualifications for membership at the NSG—even though New Delhi has not signed the Nuclear Non-proliferation Treaty (NPT) and many US allies were openly wary of such an exception.

Ironically, the opposition to India's membership in many of these groups comes not from Washington but from Beijing. At the NSG, for instance, China has been steadfast in vetoing India's entry (and at the UN Security Council too, Beijing has often opposed New Delhi's proposals and interests). But where China is not a member, there has been some success: In 2016, India became a part of the thirty-five-member Missile Technology Control Regime (MTCR), which regulates trade in missile technology.

Washington knows that its own interests would be served by India's presence in global decision-making councils—and it has repeatedly expressed that conviction. Both countries need the same sort of norms and principles to survive and thrive in the world—for the sake of their own economic and foreign policy interests. China's economic and political order, by contrast, seeks to weaken those norms, because its own economic and foreign policy interests are very different (as we saw in chapter 4).

A lack of synergy is not the challenge for India and the United States in their pursuit. The challenge, instead, is that to remake the distribution of power in international institutions, they would have to find a way to bypass Chinese presence and influence.

In many ways, India's fixation on membership is also overdone. Many people believe that India cannot be influential in international decision-making unless it is a part of these councils and boards of management. But unlike the corporate world, international politics works in *reverse*: A country needs to first become influential in order to force itself in—to make its membership indispensable to that council.

In the world of international security, many countries have exerted influence from even outside the UNSC. In the 1970s, the south-west African country of Namibia was in the throes of a war for independence, after having been under the occupation of the South African apartheid regime for years. The UNSC had long found it difficult to make South Africa behave. So, in 1977, five members of the UNSC—the US, the UK, France, Canada and West Germany—came together to form the Contact Group.* The core objective of the Contact Group was to use the combined clout of its members to mediate with the key parties concerned and bring an end to the conflict. After lengthy negotiations with the South Africans, the Namibians and other major regional powers, the Group helped reach an agreement in 1978, which formed the basis of a UN Security Council Resolution on Namibia that year. But while Canada and West Germany ceased to be part of the UNSC after 1978, their influence in the Namibian crisis did not end: The UNSC Resolution failed to resolve the conflict; so the Contact Group continued its mediation work—and remained highly influential in determining UNSC action in Namibia.

The key takeaway from the experience of Canada and West Germany in the Namibian talks is that countries can be influential in international affairs, even if they are not part of decision-making councils. But this is only possible if they increase their presence around the world and build meaningful alliances with countries which pursue common goals. In the 1970s, both Canada and West Germany were important US allies. Both of them were also far from being fence-sitters in southern Africa: Canada, for instance, had followed a policy of sanctions and embargoes of various kinds against the apartheid regime for years before it became part of the Contact Group.

In more recent times, Germany has used its presence and its strategic alliances to great effect: It was the only non-permanent member of the UNSC that played a part in the Iranian nuclear talks (called P5+1).

So membership in an international council is not by itself a magic wand for global influence. If India wants to be relevant and

---

* Canada and West Germany had been elected non-permanent members of the UNSC at the time.

important in other parts of the world, it would need political (or economic) presence there—and it would need allies who would pursue its interests.

Sugar Daddy Is a Tough Taskmaster

What is it like to be an American ally?

In 1946, shortly after World War II, Britain and America got together to sign the modern era's most comprehensive and longest-lasting intelligence-sharing agreement. The two countries all but merged their intelligence capabilities under one roof—collectively gathering and sharing top-secret sensitive information that was essential to national security (and sometimes even not so essential). In the years that followed, three more Anglophone countries joined—Canada, Australia and New Zealand—and today, this alliance is called the 'Five Eyes'.

The Five Eyes are the tightest knit of any group of countries involving the US, sharing key interests across almost every dimension. There are benefits to membership as well. Each of the Five Eyes gets privileged access to state-of-the-art intelligence capabilities, especially from Britain and America—both of which have worldwide presence and cutting-edge technology at their disposal. If India were to become part of this core circle, it would mean increased intelligence capabilities—training and technology from the top of the shelf. It would also mean access to coveted intelligence on issues from around the world—including American intelligence on things such as cross-border infiltration in Kashmir and threats along the difficult border with China. Given that weak intelligence capabilities—and a patchy record of detecting threats well in time—are among India's biggest challenges, inputs from the Five Eyes would be significantly helpful.

There are many other advantages as well: A member of the Five Eyes is the most direct beneficiary of US foreign policy influence and hard power, meaning stronger bargaining power vis-à-vis other countries, stronger national passports and more travel freedom, and increased security for their citizens overseas. It also means American security guarantees when under attack from an enemy (even, potentially, under someone like Donald Trump—a president who had watered down this commitment significantly).

The degree of support that an ally receives from the US is strategically controlled by Washington. Some European countries and NATO allies joined the Five Eyes and expanded them into forums such as the Nine Eyes and the Fourteen Eyes. But the Five Eyes still meet separately and engage in far deeper intelligence and security cooperation than the other groups. This is as close as it gets to a no-secrets friends club in international politics. And this tightness owes heavily to the uniquely deep cultural and political ties between the Five Eyes—and a genuine bonhomie that flows between the citizens themselves.

The Five Eyes are all the more extraordinary when one recognises that they are not held together by any compelling crisis or common threat. The NATO was formed due to the common threat faced by its members from the Soviets; but the Five Eyes have no equivalent. The scale of New Zealand's capabilities and the threats it faces are nowhere near those of America. Yet, New Zealand is a beneficiary of American intelligence.

Could India ever join the Five Eyes? Based on recent years, one could make the case that India and the United States are fast reaching the sort of deep cultural and political togetherness that facilitate a partnership of this kind. But India does not quite share the same rapport with the rest of the Five Eyes. (And one can even argue that India and the US are themselves not quite there yet.)

Nonetheless, even New Delhi itself is unlikely to ever want to be part of such a tightly knit core group—as full-fledged a strategic alliance with the US as one can ever have. The Five Eyes are too close to Washington for comfort. Being a US ally of this kind has benefits—but it also comes with a series of commitments. And they are not easy to fulfil: Washington has a tendency to be militaristic, and a true-blood US ally could get sucked into military intervention someplace or the other at any time. The Iraq war, for instance, was every bit Britain's war as it was America's. In the years to come, despite the strong anti-war political lobby in Washington, circumstances anywhere—from Iran to North Korea to the South China Sea—could quickly pull America into another long-drawn conflict. This is India's worst nightmare, and New Delhi will never agree to any such commitments.

The problem may not be militarism itself, but the fact that New Delhi has serious differences with Washington on the global issues which tend to pull the US into a conflict. Take Iran. As a nuclear power that has not signed the NPT itself, India has no rationale to take action against Iran for violating it. As a principle of foreign policy, India has taken the reasonable view that the NPT is unacceptable because it is inherently discriminatory. It has created a 'caste system' in international politics—five countries are given the right to maintain a nuclear arsenal while the rest have no such right. In place of such a treaty, New Delhi advocates the universal abdication of nuclear weapons by *all* countries (and it is the only nuclear power willing to give up its own nuclear weapons as part of that process).

Nonetheless, out of goodwill for Washington, India has levied sanctions on Iran in the past. But it is highly unlikely, under any circumstance, to support a military conflict with Iran. While the nuclear talks drew on endlessly, Prime Minister Manmohan Singh told President Obama that he was going to walk out at some point. More recently, Prime Minister Modi has tried to obtain exceptions from President Trump, after the latter reimposed sanctions on Iran (notably, Trump obliged and granted a temporary exception to India on oil imports from Iran and a separate, more lasting, special exception on the strategic Chabahar port project).

India also holds the fairly reasonable policy that military intervention is doomed to fail without an exit plan that leaves stability in its wake. When the West stormed into Libya to remove Muammar Gaddafi in 2011, India was among the most vocal opponents of military intervention in the UN Security Council. The Council nonetheless went ahead and authorized the invasion. What followed was the chaotic killing of the Libyan dictator and Libya's inevitable descent into lawlessness—a series of events which even spawned an aggressive and excoriating book by the then Indian ambassador to the UN, Hardeep Singh Puri.

There have been times in the past when US allies have resisted Washington's militaristic pull: New Zealand was most famously stubborn in opposition to the Iraq war in 2003. In a seminal decision, Prime Minister Helen Clark defied Washington and refused to send any troops to support the invasion. But there can also be consequences for such actions. As a New Zealander diplomat friend once complained to me, in the aftermath of the invasion, Australians who sought to work and study in the United States were rewarded with new visa concessions that were pointedly denied to New Zealand nationals.*

America's attitude towards its allies draws heavily from American exceptionalism—the belief that the United States is a chosen country with the divine mandate to be a world power. Since the fall of the Soviet Union, America has been unparalleled in its global reach and influence—and that has reinforced this idea of exceptionalism. When Washington is displeased with a country, it simply pulls out its diplomats and stops talking. Kishore Mahbubani once told me how strange this is: The very need for diplomats and diplomacy is to deal with those you have trouble

---

* This was the special E-3 visa which was created in 2005 by the Bush administration exclusively for Australian citizens as reward for their government's cooperation in Iraq.

with, he argued, not to deal with your best friends. But the message that Washington sends—either deliberately or otherwise—is that speaking to America is a privilege.

That same philosophy extends to US allies as well. Washington believes that an alliance with America is a great honour bestowed upon the ally. During his anomalous and noisy presidency, Donald Trump drew that out even further to say that America does great acts of charity towards its allies by paying for their defence or strengthening their capabilities. He also diluted America's guarantee that it will stand up for the security of its allies in times of war—the notable casualties being the Europeans and the Japanese.

Once the trust goes, there is little incentive for any country to ally with the Americans the way the Five Eyes have done for over seven decades. India will always be extremely watchful of that trend.

Building a Century-Defining Alliance

The term 'exceptionalism' is not used quite as frequently in India as in America, but the India Story makes a compelling case for exceptionalism too—a democracy weaved together out of diverse and disparate regional units, speaking hundreds of different languages and practising almost every religious faith known to man. The post-liberalization growth story has only strengthened the appeal of Indian exceptionalism—to Indians themselves, most importantly.

Just as America sees itself as the chosen land which has weathered storms to establish the world's oldest democracy, India sees itself as a one-of-a-kind story in the postcolonial world. India was among the longest sufferers of colonialism, having been under direct British rule for 200 years. It was left battered and bruised by the end of it; the British sapped India's economic wealth and resources and transported them 'from the Ganga to the Thames'.

Famines erupted at the drop of a hat across the country. Most infamously, in 1877, while millions suffered from a deadly famine, the British held a grand durbar in Delhi, replete with riches and feasts. Yet, in the aftermath of these ordeals, India erected the world's unlikeliest democracy against the least favourable of odds—and rewrote the boundaries of possibility in global political theory. By all these counts, India is a flagbearer and trendsetter in the postcolonial world—and a story of hope for what is possible by the poor and the weak.

A country with that kind of legacy cannot possibly subordinate itself to another world power—whether the United States or China. And New Delhi can never possibly be expected to give up its foreign policy independence while it seeks global leadership for itself. It cannot, for instance, go to wars at Washington's behest in far-flung places. Even while partnering the United States in the leadership of international institutions, New Delhi does not want to be a secretary to Washington. Instead, it wants to have its own identity, voice and clout.

This is a fundamental irritant in the progress of the India–US strategic alliance. Washington is already repeatedly frustrated with New Delhi's reluctance to take things to the 'next level' (which often means militarization)—including patrols in the South China Sea and military engagement in Afghanistan. Under Donald Trump, Washington had become even more demanding that its allies pull their weight on global security matters, rather than taking cover under the American military (but even Barack Obama had talked about this, albeit more politely, and it's very likely that Joe Biden will too). But whatever the merits of America's proposals, India wants to do them at its *own* pace—and by its *own* volition—rather than out of pushing and prodding from Washington. This has been India's approach to the South China Sea dispute as well: New Delhi went it alone to build a military partnership with Vietnam, for instance, even as it resisted getting pulled into

US-led coalitions. Washington might be able to goad and coerce its other allies, but not New Delhi; Indian exceptionalism means that New Delhi cannot be seen to be acting out of obligation to another power.

Yet, despite the irritants and hiccups, there is multi-partisan consensus in both countries that India and America are destined to build the 'defining partnership of the twenty-first century'. So what can that alliance look like?

Like all good relationships, this one has to be built on the most common of interests. One of India's biggest asks is stake in the leadership of international institutions. New Delhi wants a seat at the decision-making table and it wants to be part of the elite group of superpowers which lays down norms for the world through international agencies. America does not seem to be averse to this. On most political issues—and some economic issues—India's interests are the same as those of the US, which is why Washington strongly advocates India's inclusion in various forums. India's presence would add more weight to America's side of the table—to counter China and Russia, which often advocate alternative norms and principles. As a significant proportion of the future world population and economy, India would be a great asset to the maintenance of US interests in international institutions.

At some point, both sides will be keenly aware of their differences: the fact that Washington can't simply boss around New Delhi as it would expect to with its other close allies, and the fact that India's own norms and principles—particularly on economic issues—are still evolving (this is also why India is not yet a major leader in the World Bank, for instance, and why India was not considered as a participant of the Obama-led Trans-Pacific Partnership trade bloc). But given India's long-term economic and political interests—the structure of its economy and the sources of its foreign influence—New Delhi and Washington are likely to converge further and further over time in their assessments of what the world needs. The key ingredient to developing this strategic alliance, therefore, is patience—on both sides.

If America is committed to developing India into a future global power, it needs to invest in India's national power. This includes capacity-building—particularly for India's security and intelligence agencies. The two countries should engage in much deeper intelligence sharing than they already do—in fact, even to the extent to which the Five Eyes do.

For India, apart from the more obvious security benefits in South Asia, such a strong intelligence partnership will also help Indian missions around the world with critical inputs on the political, economic and social situation on the ground in the countries where they serve.* As radical as this might sound, it should not be impossible: There is no region in the world where India and America find themselves backing opposing sides in a conflict. That assessment holds true *even* for the Middle East—the world's messiest geopolitical battlefield.

America also has an important role to play in developing India's human resources and its next-generation workforce. As of 2019, over 2,00,000 Indian students were being educated in universities in the US. That number keeps climbing every year, but it's barely scratching the surface of India's vast pool of young talent. For most Indians, studying in the United States is a distant and costly dream. Quality education, therefore, must find its way to India. But even finding top-quality education in India is difficult: Only three Indian universities ranked in the top 200 in the world in 2020–21, and capacity even in these institutes is woefully limited. There is vast potential for cooperation between the two countries in bridging this gap—with the goal of inculcating a culture of

---

*   This is possible if Indian and American missions in various countries (say, Syria or Iraq) collaborate on intelligence gathering and analysis. Why is this important for India? More about that in the next chapter.

research and innovation, particularly to develop Indian industry (a unique strength of American higher education). On a related note, there is a need to develop India's ability to conduct research and development in the defence field—to innovate and build state-of-the-art military capacity.

To be fair, Washington has already walked a fair distance on most of these issues. India now enjoys privileges of defence technology transfer and joint development which few US allies enjoy. And almost every bilateral summit between the two countries takes this forward—with the aim of strengthening India's military capacity, particularly vis-à-vis the Chinese. Even on the issue of education, American schools have been forthcoming. One of India's top business schools—the Indian School of Business—was established with support from Wharton and Kellogg. In the 2010s, top US universities began opening research centres across India: the University of Chicago in New Delhi, Virginia Tech in Chennai, and Harvard Business School in Mumbai. In the New Education Policy (NEP) that was rolled out in 2020, the Indian government promised a framework to allow top foreign universities to open their own campuses in India. But this is a promise that has long struggled to overcome political and bureaucratic hurdles in India, even under previous governments.

The onus lies more on New Delhi's side—to turn America into its closest partner in building India's national power and using American foreign policy influence for the cause of India's rise as a global power. First things first, India needs to start pulling its weight and cooperating with the US on common action around the world. Take Afghanistan. In the past, India's security and intelligence relationship with America has been derailed by Washington's alliance with Pakistan in Afghanistan. In the past, reports have suggested that close ties between the CIA and Pakistan's spy agency, the ISI, have hindered intelligence sharing between India and the US, particularly on Kashmir. But much of this stems from India's unwillingness to play a more meaningful and influential security role on the ground. Pakistan's leverage over various militant groups makes Islamabad indispensable to Washington (on occasions when the US has ticked off the Pakistanis, NATO forces in Afghanistan have found their supply lines blocked). New Delhi has simply been unable to replace Pakistan—or counter its influence. But with NATO forces now withdrawing, India has a responsibility to find ways to fill the security vacuum—something that would fulfil the common interests of both India and the US.

Afghanistan is a tricky game, and India cannot be fully blamed for its constraints in that country. But in other parts of the world, New Delhi has certainly been a laggard—particularly in fulfilling proactive roles that would uphold security and stability. India is not averse to military action around the world: It has long been one of the top troop contributors to UN peacekeeping, putting boots on the ground in some very violent conflict zones. But it must be willing to do more of the same with the US, particularly in areas where there are very clear common interests (which is almost everywhere). India should ally US forces more proactively in the South China Sea and the Indian Ocean—where the two countries face threats of intimidation from China and need freedom of navigation and trade. Conflict-ridden Africa—an important emerging market—is another region for common action on security.

New Delhi does not do enough of all this, but it isn't true that it does nothing at all. In the Indian Ocean and the South China Sea, for instance, India has now signed a series of deals with various countries—from Seychelles to Singapore—for military cooperation. But New Delhi suffers from an allergy for similar military alliances with the United States. Some of this is a Cold War hangover and the need to show the developing world that India is its own country. But much of it is also the fear that Washington would bully New Delhi if there is a formal military alliance. New Zealand's experience with the Iraq war reinforces those fears.

But Washington's outreach so far points to the fact that India is not New Zealand; with its size and potential future influence, India is much more important to America in upholding American interests worldwide. That is the only reason that America has been willing to do so much heavy lifting on India's behalf—from endorsements at the NSG, to excusing New Delhi from levying sanctions on Iran. With no other country in the world does America have a relationship on the other side's terms. But in the India–US relationship, it increasingly seems that Washington is willing to have strategic cooperation on New Delhi's terms.

6

The New Guard

The World That India Should Build

In the globalized world, it isn't merely goods, services and people
that travel the world. Viruses do too. The year 2020 opened with
a new nightmare infection making its way around the world. The
novel coronavirus—scientifically called COVID-19—began its
journey from a seafood market in the town of Wuhan in China.
On New Year's Eve 2019, the World Health Organization said
that it was informed of a cluster of pneumonia cases in that city.
Since then, the virus has spread like wildfire.

The world has seen a few epidemics in the recent past—
Ebola, for instance, in 2014, and SARS a decade earlier—but
none of them spread as quickly as COVID-19. SARS was largely
contained within East Asia, while Ebola affected West Africa
the most. But within just two months of the epidemic making
headlines, over *100 countries* had seen a case of COVID-19 in
their midst. By that time itself, the most affected countries were
as diverse and far away as China, Iran, Italy and the United
States. Global hub cities were the worst hit early on—Dubai,

New York, Milan and so on—taking the brunt of hosting visitors from around the world.

Epidemics and public health emergencies make the strongest case of all for international cooperation. The presence of a virus anywhere in the world can be a threat to people everywhere else. In 2013–14, the Ebola outbreak is said to have originated in the small, remote village of Meliandou in Guinea—nestled in the interior areas of the country and at least 400 km away from the nearest major city, Monrovia in Liberia. Yet, the epidemic spread far enough to cause a death across the Atlantic in the United States.

If Ebola showed that gaps in the public health and hygiene systems in remote corners of the world can thus result in severe consequences even in more developed countries, the COVID-19 pandemic has shown that those consequences can travel very rapidly around the world. Globalized cities, which depend on international economic transactions, are the most vulnerable—and by extension, any country that does any trade or transaction through them is at risk. The only way to ensure stability in the globalized economy is to partner countries everywhere in meeting their developmental challenges. That means more international cooperation, not less. International organizations must receive strong support from all global powers in drawing out and implementing policies and norms to strengthen public systems worldwide. Countries must be more transparent about their shortcomings and needs—and other countries must be more willing to support them in fixing those gaps. This is not just about health—it is also about overall resilience across nations, whether in response to climate change, security threats or migration.

But in recent years, the world has been decidedly travelling in the opposite direction—away from multilateral cooperation rather than towards it. For over half a century, America has sponsored and maintained the international network of norms and institutions which have kept governments, businesses and people around the world connected—precisely to tide over such challenges in international development. Yet, under Donald Trump, that era was put under severe threat. America was fast withdrawing from its leadership role: The Trump administration took a sledgehammer to the UN and its agencies, and cut spending on diplomacy while diverting those funds towards the military. Trump also diluted Washington's commitment to its allies on their security and development. The result has been an anarchic, multipolar world order, with competing global powers, heightened nationalism, more selfish action and less cooperation. As Ian Bremmer, the inimitable *Time* columnist and commentator, puts it: We are in a 'G–Zero World'.

For India, the 'G–Zero World' presents both challenges and opportunities. India has been one of the biggest beneficiaries of globalization—and, by extension, the international institutions which make globalization possible. In particular, it has been a free-rider on American norms: including the promotion of basic rights and freedoms around the world for its own businesses and citizens abroad, and the proliferation of liberal policies on trade and immigration to help its own economy develop.

America's withdrawal under Trump meant the potential dawn of a rebellious world order pushed by China and Russia—countries that do not share these norms and have taken initiatives that have threatened them. But even if Joe Biden now reverses Trump's isolationist policies, it's fair to believe that America will no longer play the same unilateral role that it once did in sustaining these international institutions. Even progressives in America have long believed that Washington was stretching itself out too thin through its foreign policy efforts.

But the opportunity for New Delhi is that it is now large enough and consequential enough to be a solution to these problems. For decades, India played the role of a rule-taker in a unipolar world, owing to its own limited national power. But now, as one of the rising poles in the new multipolar world, India has the opportunity to become a *rule-maker*—and to uphold the norms, principles and policies worldwide which fulfil its interests as a democratic society and a globalized economy.

To become a rule-maker, India needs to build its political presence and capital worldwide—in other words, it needs what we have been calling 'influence' throughout this book. The best way for New Delhi to gain global influence is to be the solution to the gaping holes in the international system. It has to become the flagbearer of a style of international cooperation that works for countries around the world.

The steps that New Delhi must take in this quest for global leadership cannot be achieved overnight—but it is a journey that India should soon embark upon. That begins with a more proactive foreign policy attitude; one which also fulfils the national interests of *other* countries rather than just India's alone.

The Delhi Consensus

I have spent much of my early career as a policy consultant, working in the Middle East and helping governments in that region learn from the rest of the world. My projects have included strengthening state institutions, learning best practices in various policymaking domains, and implementing international norms in different areas of governance within countries in the Middle East. This is a most extraordinary phenomenon. For generations, the Middle East—and the Arabian Peninsula in particular—has been among the most insular regions in the world. The Gulf states, led by Saudi Arabia, have long reflexively viewed foreign ideas as a threat. Ruling monarchs often take an aggressive 'my way or the highway' approach to domestic governance. The irony is not lost on those who are now called to help: Some Western consultants joke that the last time a foreigner was given so much credence was in the days of Lawrence of Arabia.

All that seems to be changing—at least on apolitical issues. Driven by both political and economic incentives to pull his kingdom out of ultra-conservatism, Saudi Arabia's crown prince, Mohammed bin Salman, is increasingly looking to foreigners for help. In recent years, Saudi Arabia's volatile oil economy has begun to lose confidence in itself. Oil prices have gone up and down—also suffering due to China's slowdown and internal economic restructuring. America's newfound energy independence has only made things worse.

Prince Mohammed knows that if his reign is to survive, he would have to do much more than just drill crude oil out of the ground: He would have to build a modern economy. In order to do this, the prince is trying to woo foreign investment, to a country where the non-oil private sector is virtually non-existent and few foreigners have ever been welcome. That means a whole host of reforms, from rebranding the country's ultra-conservative and regressive image, to developing a society in which foreigners feel secure investing, living and working.

An under-skilled and inefficient bureaucratic machinery must now begin fulfilling activities which it has not previously had to deal with. Saudi government officials are not used to collecting robust data on the economy, for instance, because nobody ever asks them questions at home. But foreign investors are not so easy to please. The bureaucracy now needs to learn to effectively regulate a market economy, build a more modern financial system, and govern more transparently.

Saudi Arabia's ambitious reform and modernization plans have spawned an unprecedented consulting mega-market. In 2013, consulting firms such as McKinsey, Kearney, BCG and others generated market revenues of just under $2 billion. By 2019, the industry was making well over $3 billion—growing at a minimum of 6 per cent every year.[1] Much of this is in the public sector: Projects include advising the government in restructuring outdated state institutions, learning best practices from other countries, training government officials, and supporting policymaking in technical areas such as healthcare and defence. The image makeover is just as important as substantive reform: Saudi Arabia wants to tell the world that it is trying to modernize itself.

Saudi Arabia's needs for international support in policy development are shared by many countries in the developing world, but few have such hefty resources to pay global consulting firms. Countries have a particular need for the joint development of norms of governance in more technologically advanced and ever-evolving areas, such as cybersecurity. In the run-up to the G20 summit in 2020 in Riyadh, the Saudis sought to conduct several conferences and events to build international consensus on issues such as cybersecurity and the digital economy. Some of these events are aimed at getting outside perspectives on how Saudi Arabia can build a robust modern economy for itself.

What the world needs is an organizer for a grand global effort at sharing lessons and experiences in development—to make norms for modern-day governance. In the post-WWII world, American international institutions lectured the world on the basic building blocks of a modern economy and society; they established standards on such things as airline safety and telecommunications. Today, the world needs an organizer to launch an effort to co-create such norms and standards for new frontiers of policymaking in the digital economy. It also needs an organizer who can help the developing world strengthen its public systems (especially in the post-COVID-19 paradigm). In the consulting world, the term used for all these things is 'capacity-building'.

India has many advantages that would help it in fulfilling this role: For a developing economy, it already has a sizable labour pool that is remarkably well skilled in key areas of the modern digital economy. It also has fairly mature and internationally credible state institutions—and these have often formed a template for similar institutions in the rest of the developing world, owing to similar social and economic environments in those countries. The Indian Election Commission, for instance, has served as an independent and credible foreign observer for elections in as many as ten countries around the world, including Egypt, Venezuela, Mexico, Sri Lanka, Bhutan and Cambodia.[2] In 2006, the Reserve Bank of India joined hands with the International Monetary Fund to launch the India–IMF Training Programme for central bankers from South Asia and East Africa.

New Delhi also has some basic infrastructure in place to coordinate such capacity-building efforts worldwide: As early as 1964, Prime Minister Lal Bahadur Shastri established the Indian Technical and Economic Cooperation (ITEC) Programme to assist fellow developing countries in standing up on their feet. Among other support, the ITEC provides partners with training on a wide range of contemporary policy issues, deputes Indian experts abroad on request, and provides even professional consultancy services on capacity-building—not unlike what private consulting firms do in the Middle East. The Indian government also engages in sharing best practices in governance with partner countries through various forums.

But a lot of what India currently does is bilateral in scope—not multilateral. New Delhi needs to expand its bilateral cooperation programmes into multilateral ones: Build partnerships with allies which bear similar political and economic interests across regions; engage in the multilateral development of solutions to global policy challenges; and share lessons and experiences with each other to progressively strengthen public systems and state institutions worldwide. A multilateral partnership has several foreign policy benefits over bilateral initiatives: It is more visible to the world, more impactful in international decision-making, and more substantive to each individual member by including inputs and resources from a larger membership.

Think of China's BRI. Chinese assistance to the developing world is not new; some African partners received aid for infrastructure as early as during the days of Mao himself. But up until the BRI, these were done on a bilateral basis and were hence limited in impact on the world stage. Xi's foreign policy genius is in tying these together into a grand multilateral scheme—branding the outcomes of one project in one country as benefits that would accrue to another country elsewhere.

India needs to do the same: Build a grand coalition with allies from various regions and set up a global knowledge-sharing and capacity-building network for more enlightened governance. The forum can host countries from around the world to develop solutions to several challenges that are specific to the developing world. Lessons may be borrowed and shared from every part of the globe. These can then take the shape of global norms and standards for policymaking—resulting in a kind of 'Delhi Consensus'. Each country can benefit from the inputs and resources of other member countries—with India as the main organizer and promoter of the forum. The alliance can even conduct projects and initiatives—similar to ITEC's—to implement these ideas and build more effective public systems around the world. And through its weight, it can influence norm-building and decision-making at the UN.

Such a global coalition to promote 'good governance' would also help India with its own domestic development. Despite its strides in recent decades, India still struggles with the delivery of many basic public services. Institutionalized corruption is a long-running complaint. Borrowing ideas that have worked in other parts of the world through such a forum would not be a bad approach at all.

At present, forums such as the G20 and the World Economic Forum play these roles in promoting ideas for good governance. But they are either too small or too exclusive to enjoy sufficient international legitimacy. More importantly, the developing world is often left out of leadership in these elite clubs—and they are the most important beneficiaries of the exercise. An India-led forum could help plug these gaps.

There is, however, one great inadequacy in this plan to strengthen public systems worldwide: Capacity-building needs a willing government in place. But how do you build capacity if there is no stable, reliable or willing government in power?

An Eye for an Eye

The most threatening crisis in international security is often characterized as 'terrorism', but terrorism is merely a symptom of a much larger, more universal crisis. The most threatening crisis today is, in fact, the proliferation of protests and rebellions across the world. From Hong Kong to Lebanon, Venezuela and beyond, countries are suffering from debilitating violence and civil strife because governments have lost legitimacy in the eyes of their disenchanted people. And like a virus, the crisis spreads—from country to country—leaving destruction behind. The Arab Spring left big political vacuums in its wake, which were filled by lawlessness and terrorism—and it all started with disenchantment among citizens who saw their rulers as being illegitimate.

This is not a sudden or new phenomenon. Since it won independence from European colonists in the 1960s, Africa has seen over 200 civil wars, particularly in the central, western and northern regions. Much of this has taken place away from the spotlight of the world's cameras, but it hasn't gone unnoticed in international politics. A significant portion of the UN Security Council's work is on Africa (as much as two-thirds, according to one former chief of UN peacekeeping). The script—from the Central African Republic to Côte d'Ivoire and the Congo—is often similar. Tinpot dictators come to power as paper democrats and begin centralizing power. Invariably, the dictators would favour their own clan or tribe—appointing them to senior government positions and giving them control over national resources. In doing so, the dictator turns all state institutions into pliant entities—from the military to the judiciary and even the election commission. And these institutions, in turn, help the dictator consolidate his position.

Dictators often use the military, in particular, to entrench their own rule: So long as they control the folks with the guns, dictators feel immune to all threats, including from other state institutions. In his book, *The Looting Machine*, Tom Burgis of the *Financial Times* wrote of the example of Angola in 2013: Even though that country was in peace at the time, Burgis writes, the government spent 18 per cent of its budget on the military and police forces—almost 40 per cent more than it spent on health and education combined.[3]

You might have already guessed the inevitable outcome: Rival clans and tribes feel alienated, having little or no voice in politics, governance or even the economy. This kind of obscene centralization of power makes everything worse in poor countries. In most of these countries, individuals have few resources to launch their own private enterprises; most secure jobs are in the government and the public sector—and are thereby dominated by the ruling clan. People are dependent on government institutions for even basic provisions such as food and water. Worse, the disenchanted tribes have little recourse or opportunity to fight back, with democratic institutions firmly in the grip of the dictator. The result: a civil war. The disenchanted tribes organize themselves around a rebel leader, form militias and storm the capital city.

The victory of the rebels in a civil war does not necessarily end the vicious cycle. When in power, the rebels follow the same political culture that their predecessors did—once again monopolizing the state and its economic resources, and once again creating a disenchanted population. In 2013, Muslim rebels—called

the Seleka—grabbed power in the Christian-dominated Central
African Republic, following years of marginalization. But their
own tyranny only induced a counter-rebellion from a coalition
of Christian militias, called the Anti-balaka. The deep mistrust
between the two groups continues to frustrate international efforts
at peace and power-sharing, even to this day.

The vicious civil war cycle is a great poverty trap for many
countries—and its impact on the rest of the world is often
underplayed. Most efforts at development and improvement in
governance occur among relatively stable states (the India-led Delhi
Consensus alliance that I described in the previous section, for
instance, will likely be dominated by stable states, if it were ever to
see the light of day). But this is not sufficient for global leadership.
There are many moral reasons why the world—or world powers—
should not overlook conflict-ridden fragile states: They are home
to millions of people who deserve to be part of the modern world;
they too deserve the peace and prosperity that citizens in relatively
stable states enjoy. Any world power should address their interests
and concerns, if it is to be worthy of global leadership.

But there are also compelling realist reasons not to overlook them.
Generations of talent and economic potential are lost to violence in
civil wars. Of all the world's regions, Africa has the fastest-growing
population and the youngest demographics: According to the World
Economic Forum, nineteen of the world's twenty youngest countries
are in Africa (Niger has a median age of just *fifteen years*).[4] But since
schools are largely closed and dysfunctional during a war—and well-
meaning NGOs and charities cannot bring quality education to a
battlefield—millions of young children find their lives and dreams
lost. As one political scientist put it to me at Columbia, 'There could
be doctors out there who might have found a cure to cancer, but we
never managed to educate them and give them a chance.'

Global epidemics have a high chance of originating in these
countries too—Ebola being a prime example. They have limited

public health infrastructure and low levels of hygiene (and, during a civil war, even in relatively richer countries, these are hardly the primary concerns for most people). Potential epidemics are therefore easily undetected, for want of facilities. Yet, in the globalized world, even a war-torn state is not an isolated state: soldiers, peacekeepers and humanitarian workers from around the world travel back and forth through these countries—and if a novel infection were to originate here, it would travel everywhere with them.

Then, there is global terrorism, which often uses political vacuums as a launchpad. In Mali, Libya, Somalia, Syria and Iraq, civil wars often had little to do with global terrorist networks when they began. Yet, they soon fell victim to them. The lawlessness of a broken state is a perfect breeding ground for terrorist groups: There is already plenty of anger, chaos and youthful militancy to tap into among the local population. Everybody knows about how ISIS installed itself in Syria and Iraq, but few know about how they travelled the world from there—going to places such as Libya and Mali by making use of local lawlessness. According to a 2016 Crisis Group report, there were—at the time—anywhere between 2000 and 10,000 ISIS fighters in Libya, having grown exponentially through an influx of militants from the Middle East.[5] The Al Qaeda and its affiliates in Mali similarly recruited thousands of anti-Gaddafi Libyan rebels after the fall of that regime. Through organized crime in lawless countries, global terrorist networks often enrich themselves to launch attacks in other parts of the world.

But if the world wanted to break this cycle of violence, how can it do that?

Sensing Impending Doom

Even before the Arab Spring came to Syria, the writing was on the wall. There was little to suggest that Bashar al-Assad was different enough from Hosni Mubarak or Muammar Gaddafi to escape the wrath of his people.

For several years, Syria stumbled from coup to coup until Bashar's father, Hafez al-Assad, crowned himself president in 1971 and established a one-party state. An ophthalmologist who was educated in London and married to a Brit, the junior Assad came to power in 2000, raising hopes among his people of democratic reform—he was young, seemingly westernized and often spoke of democratizing his country. Yet, the reforms never came. Just a year into office, Assad crushed a nascent democratic movement. Worse, he continued his father's legacy of politically favouring his own clan—the minority Shia Alawites—at the expense of the rest. Crony capitalism ruled over the economy and those close to the president enjoyed first rights over any national resources.

For an aspirational middle-class Syrian population, the abuse was going too far. By mid-2011, as they watched the Egyptians and Libyans successfully revolt against their own despots, Syrians too took to the streets, asking for a democracy in place of Assad's sham one-party republic. Assad responded with disproportionate force (according to some US reports, he is even suspected of having used chemical weapons on his own people)—and soon, Syria became the epicentre of a horrifying refugee crisis. Among the most iconic and heart-wrenching images of the catastrophe was that of three-year-old Alan Kurdi, who drowned in the Mediterranean Sea while trying to escape the violence, and washed up dead on the Turkish coast. Kurdi was not even born when the protests first started in Syria. Yet, he did not escape it.

But all of this could have been seen coming for a while. Syria exhibited all the elements of a problem state even before the Arab Spring came: marginalization of some sections and clans in society; a centralized one-party state which monopolized economic resources; and dysfunctional state institutions which did not credibly provide democratic recourse to the people. Apart from higher income levels, there was not much fundamentally different between Syria and, say, the Central African Republic.

Once it began, there was only one of two ways in which the Arab Spring was going to go in Syria: one, Assad gets overthrown like Gaddafi did and the vacuum is filled by hodgepodge rebel militias, or two, Assad doubles down on his opponents and centralizes his despotic regime even more.

In the end, Syria went the second way, but Africa's experience suggests that the rebel militias would not have necessarily established a stable state themselves. In all likelihood, the fall of Assad may have merely induced infighting among the rebels, because they were nowhere near organized enough to run a political party or a government. (That is what happened in Libya, for instance.) The lawlessness may have even been exploited by terrorist groups. (This was ISIS' strategy.) If Syria were to have been 'luckier' and one of the rebel groups had prevailed over the radicals in establishing a government of its own, then the cycle of despotism would likely have continued under the new regime—just as it often does in Africa's recurring civil wars.

The reason civil wars become a recurring cycle is two-fold: First, most rebellions are largely sporadic and unorganized. As a result, the only rebels who are politically organized enough to form a government are those that already exist as parties or militias. And these are typically organized along the lines of identity—clans, tribes, sects and so on. Second, since these organized rebel groups often take part in the civil war out of resentment against their own marginalization, their only objective is to undo (or *reverse*) the marginalization in their own favour. As a result, the new despots simply replace the old despots and retain the centralized, authoritarian political system just as they had inherited it. And in a few years, the whole thing begins all over again.

Governments become stable and viable when a wider cross-section of their country's population considers them legitimate.

In other words, the public must believe that the government *deserves* to rule and that it is not marginalizing anybody maliciously. Advanced democracies are often stable because the elected government wins the vote of a significant portion of the population—and if the public loses faith in it, they can always vote it out after a while. Autocratic regimes do not have this luxury: They have no way of proving their legitimacy to their people—and owing to restrictions on freedom of speech and expression, the people have no means within the system to make themselves heard when they are unhappy. As a result, when the government loses legitimacy among the people, it has no way of making amends, and transfer of power must necessarily be violent. That is why, for all its chaos and noise, democracy is often considered the most stable form of government. As Winston Churchill put it, 'Democracy is the worst form of government, except for all those other forms.'

Building a Democracy

Let me caveat these bold, sweeping statements with a disclaimer: None of this is an invitation to airdrop democracy around the world.

That is what America's first instinct has often been—and it has invariably failed. There are few more legendary failures than the one in Iraq: a case study of bad foreign policy that will likely make it into textbooks on international relations for some time to come. According to a BBC report, America lost nearly 4500 personnel between 2003 and 2011, following the invasion to remove Saddam Hussein. That wasn't even the worst of it: The same report quotes numerous studies which estimate the loss of Iraqi civilian lives in the hundreds of thousands.[6]

But believe it or not, the military conquest was in fact the easier part of the operation. The harder challenge was to leave behind a stable government which would reflect the aspirations of the Iraqi people better—and prevent a civil war down the road. As much as one might criticize the American invasion of Iraq, it is hard to argue that Iraq was going to survive under Saddam Hussein through the Arab Spring. Like Assad's Syria, Saddam's Iraq was another problem state: He had politically marginalized the sizeable Shia population; set up a corrupt, crony capitalist state; and brutalized anybody who attempted to oppose him. It was not unimaginable that Baghdad would have been filled with protestors in 2011—and turned into yet another Syria.

Yet, in its efforts to bring freedom to Iraq, Washington only brought more chaos. In its wake, it left behind an even worse problem state. In the quest to remove Saddam, the US removed *all traces* of his party itself; anybody who had served, worked or occupied positions in the Saddam regime or his army were purged shortly after the invasion. The result was near-complete marginalization of the Sunni Arab population, which had dominated the Saddam regime. When elections were held by the US-led coalition, Sunnis often boycotted them; and the few Sunnis who did enter the political system found themselves left out of senior government positions. In 2011, after US troops left the country, Prime Minister Nouri al-Maliki began an open crackdown on prominent Sunni politicians—including his vice president, Tariq al-Hashemi.[7] By 2012, sure enough, Iraqi protestors were out on the streets, jumping on the Arab Spring bandwagon. The disenchantment of Sunnis in the country drew terrorist groups to the region and spawned the rise of ISIS.

America spent eight painful years in Iraq and billions of dollars towards state-building. Why did it fail to build a stable democracy? The problem with democracy is that it cannot simply be airdropped into alien territory by holding an election. Democracies need much more than just elections; they need the nurturing of a 'democratic culture'. A stable democracy requires a Constitution that enjoys widespread legitimacy among the people and separates powers across professional state institutions. It requires a truly independent judiciary and a conscientious civil service. The police and military forces must be politically (and ethnically) neutral. The central bank must be independent and professional. The press must be free and reflect a diversity of opinions. And all of these institutions must work to provide recourse to the people against the excesses of those in power. More importantly—they must do that with impartiality towards all sections of the population.

Above all, the citizenry must be willing to live together in a single nation and trust that their collective democratic decision-making will be wise and fair. Most people underestimate how difficult this last bit is; in countries like Iraq, national identity stems from the barrel of the dictator's gun, and once he was gone, people became more Shia or Sunni than Iraqi. In 2015, a *Washington Post* report found that only 40 per cent of Iraqis polled by a survey identified themselves as 'Iraqi above all'.[8] This is extremely dangerous in a democracy. Democracy can result in chaos and violence if the citizens are not willing to live with each other under one unifying national identity. In countless countries, from Sri Lanka to the Philippines, democratic institutions—even professional and mature ones—have been used by the majority community to oppress, marginalize and silence the minorities, all in the name of having won the popular vote in the elections.

Building a stable democracy takes *decades* and its processes cannot be forced upon a country all at once. Think about India. By the time India declared itself an independent democracy in 1947, it had already gone through more than sixty years of gradual democratization. The Indian National Congress was one in a long line of political associations in British India, which connected people together and brought about a culture of civic participation and democratic discussion. Among the Congress' members were political leaders such as Dadabhai Naoroji who had even held a seat in the British Parliament in London.

As time went by, the British government tried to placate the agitating Indian political organizations with small concessions: First, legislative assemblies were established across India to advise the British government's executive, and its members were nominated by the colonists. Then, a few seats were set aside for election by a restricted Indian electorate. Over time, the concessions became larger and larger, even if much more gradually than the Indian freedom fighters demanded.

There was also the genius of Gandhi. Mahatma Gandhi is known quite rightly for his philosophy of non-violence, but he also played another under-appreciated role: nation-building. Before him, politics was largely the preserve of the aristocratic. But under Gandhi, the Congress took its message of a new Indian nation down to the grassroots. It helped create a relatively cohesive national identity out of an extremely diverse crowd: Gandhi's efforts fulfilled the interests of farmers in Bihar as much as it did the industrialists in Bombay.*

By 1947, India's leaders—and its people—by and large knew exactly what they were doing. The big transformative change came in the form of universal adult franchise (British-run elections did not allow all Indians above eighteen to vote). But elections themselves were not an alien concept. Neither was the idea of civilian political organization; there were already plenty of civilian political parties in India which had become comfortable with the idea of democratic politics. Indian leaders too had years of experience in democratic debates and discussions on public policy within the chambers of British India's dummy assemblies. And the

---

* That was later sullied by Partition. But remember: After 1947, it was the supposedly homogenous Muslim state of Pakistan that suffered a second partition—not India's hodgepodge nation.

absence of violence meant that there were no armed militias to dominate the civilian leadership.

Contrast this to the typical run-of-the-mill uprising against a despotic regime. When unorganized protestors rise against a dictator, they generally lack a political organization like the Indian National Congress. Therefore, there is no direction or cohesion given to the many disconnected voices among the protestors. The revolution is oftentimes violent, which means that the dominant political forces are—not civilian organizations—but armed militias. The worst of it is that the armed radicals are the best organized group—which means that when the uprising is over and the dictator has been removed, the power vacuum is inevitably filled by them. But being armed militias, these outfits have limited experience in (or inclination towards) the civilian governance of a country. Their first instinct, instead, is to quell and crush.

Worse, there are no democratic institutions to help transition the country from war to peace. And the lack of political organization during the uprising means that there is no one to take responsibility for this state-building—no Nehru or Mandela, to put it simply.

The development of a democratic culture is simply too much work for a country to do when it has no one willing to do it. The irony of India's experience is that its efforts at building a democratic culture came under a tyrannical regime. If the British had packed their bags and left after the violent uprising of 1857, India would likely have crumbled like Syria or Iraq; there were no inclusive or multicultural political organizations, no democratic culture and no cohesive national identity. That is what happened in Iraq after Saddam Hussein was removed: The Americans found out that there was no cohesive nation under the dictator, and once he was gone, the power vacuum was simply filled by those who had opposed him. There were still no robust state institutions to check *their* excesses. And there were no civilian leaders or political organizations to bring about an inclusive process to build those institutions.*

Before the Arab Spring came to Syria, there was a small window of opportunity for the world's powers to learn their lessons from Iraq (and India). To maintain political stability in Syria, the international community should have sought the gradual democratization of Syria *under Assad*—much like India experienced under British rule. The key role of the dictator in this exercise is to uphold law and order. Having done that, at first, he should have been coerced into allowing freer press in some contained fashion, before expanding that freedom over time. Political parties should have been allowed some space to develop over time. The legislative assembly should similarly have been democratized gradually, as in British India.

All this sounds too idealistic, given that a revolution was just around the corner. But there were incentives on all sides to pursue such a path. For one, Assad had much more to lose by suffering a revolution than by gently placating his protestors in order to stay on in power peacefully (this was the same calculation that the British made in India, in fact). It would not have taken too much diplomatic effort on the part of countries such as the United States (and India) to convey that rationale to him. If protestors saw Assad making good on his promises early on, many of them may have been discouraged from disrupting their own lives by taking to the streets; indeed, the protests only got *worse* when Assad began cracking down violently.

---

* A very important clarification: This is not an appraisal of the tyrannical British regime. India's democratization happened only because it had wise and educated leaders who demanded the right things from the British—the right to organize politically, an assembly to discuss and deliberate policy, and legal frameworks to uphold the rights of Indians. This was the wisdom of the Indians, not the British. Left to their whims, the British would have doubled down on oppression rather than build an Indian state.

For Assad, there would also have been the appeal of building a legacy: Ever since he came to power, Assad had been promising democratic reform, without ever seeing the need for it. Here was a chance for him to walk his country through a years-long process of democratization, without even fully giving up his own political influence. (In fact, chances are that his democratization—as it yielded fruit—would only have endeared the public towards him over time.)

Demagogues love a good name. There is no better way to win a good name than to build a nation that would last long after you are gone.

The Dirty P-Word

Over the years, India has conveyed its intentions to fill this state-building gap in international politics. Everybody knows about India's efforts in Afghanistan, but there have also been other initiatives. In 2012, the Indian foreign ministry established the Development Partnership Administration (DPA), bringing together specialized technical, legal and other skills to implement aid projects around the world. The DPA was also tasked with the implementation of projects under the ITEC, which sought to build the capacity of public systems in various countries, among other things. India has not shied away from backing democracy either: Along with the United States, India has long been a regular and generous contributor to the United Nations Democracy Fund, which is meant to help post-conflict states build credible democratic institutions after years of violence. India has been especially useful to the Afghans in developing their fragile democracy so far—advising state institutions such as the election commission, building Parliament, and even nurturing a nascent free press.

This is a reasonable policy: People around the world look up to the credibility and inspiration of India's democratic success.

And India's efforts to strengthen nation-states and make them stable are important to its global influence. It's a classic case of representing the interests of people in another country and thereby making your own welfare and national power important to them. This is why India's voice is well regarded by political leaders in Afghanistan; New Delhi's influence has directly benefited their efforts to establish a stable state to stand up to the Taliban, and therefore, politicians like Ashraf Ghani, Hamid Karzai and Amrullah Saleh do not often contradict India's narrative or advice on even sensitive political matters.

But outside Afghanistan, relying entirely on the United Nations to rebuild broken states is not enough. In typical circumstances, the task of building democratic institutions after a civil war is left to the UN. In countries like Liberia and the Central African Republic, the end of a civil war saw the withdrawal of UN peacekeeping troops, who were replaced by UN political and legal advisers. UN advisers serve as consultants to the new post-war transition government in building democratic institutions. The UN term for this activity is 'peacebuilding'—and its goal is to help break the vicious cycle of recurring civil wars and instability.

But as we know, peacebuilding is an inherently murky political process; the winners of the civil war—who typically dominate the new regime—are inclined to monopolize and centralize the nation all over again. Oftentimes, the UN's considered and patient advice is therefore ignored—and as an international organization, the UN does not have the political power to coerce the new government into behaving. Coercion can only come through the collective action of the world's leading powers. But owing to the absence of conflict (until it recurs again), the UN Security Council does not take any action—instead opting to focus resources on firefighting.

In recent years, the UN's leadership—starting from the secretary general—has been trying to push world powers towards prevention over firefighting. In 2017, Secretary General Antonio

Guterres wrote, 'By prevention, I mean doing everything we can to help countries to avert the outbreak of crises that take a high toll in human lives and undermine the institutions and capacities needed to achieve peace and development.'[9] In Syria, that would mean doing what I previously prescribed—gradual democratization and state-building before the protests exploded into a civil war.

World powers—including aspiring ones—should supplement the UN's peacebuilding and prevention efforts with political and diplomatic support. If New Delhi is looking for an opportunity to boost its relevance and influence in international politics, this is a fertile area to cash in on. In Syria, for instance, India could have pushed Washington to join in an effort to apply diplomatic pressure on Assad before it got too late. Across Africa, where civil wars recur, India has the opportunity to become a political leader and global organizer in the effort to support the UN's peacebuilding efforts—to goad the new government to behave responsibly.

In practical terms, this could mean setting up a special political mission in that country, along with allies, to exert diplomatic pressure on the transition government when necessary—and to play a positive role in the more political aspects of democracy-building. The inputs of members of the 'Delhi Consensus' coalition, which I described earlier, could be used to supplement the UN's capacity-building efforts.

But all this means that New Delhi has to take positions in a conflict; it cannot take the steps prescribed here by sitting on the fence. That requirement is a significant problem. Politics is a dirty word in the Indian psyche. That goes for both the domestic and international arenas: Barring political dynasties, most Indian parents and families would not instinctively support the political ambitions of the young men or women in their households. On the international stage, similarly, Indira Gandhi's cynical, inward turn has persisted. In 2013, one of the then senior functionaries of India's Development Partnership Administration, P.S. Raghavan pointed out: 'Unlike the aid of Western donors, which is often conditional on recipient government policies regarding governance, human rights, etc., India's development assistance is demand-driven and does not constrain the sovereignty of its partners in any way.' He then added, 'Indeed, India sees this as one of the defining features of South-South cooperation.'[10] It is indeed a defining feature of the cooperation that India drives, but it is a most unfortunate feature all the same—even compromising India's own interests and influence. It means that whatever India does, it will not use its coercive strength against a government—even Assad's, for that matter.

India's uncompromising devotion to sovereignty stems in part from the morals of the postcolonial era. Nehru was anything but a fence-sitter, but he often built his foreign policy activism around the maintenance of sovereignty. Remember, when the Congo plunged into a crisis back then, Nehru supported the Congolese government against the Western-backed rebels whom it was fending off. And he succeeded: While the West wanted the UN to stand by, Nehru managed to get the UN to intervene in the government's favour—and India personally led the peacekeeping troops to victory.

In the 1950s and 1960s, this policy made some sense: Newly independent states were wary of continued intervention from their erstwhile colonial powers and the respect for sovereignty was therefore constructed to protect them from such exploitation. But in the years after Nehru, India's commitment to sovereignty has become more a symbol of its fence-sitting on burning international issues than a symbol of Nehru's activist foreign policy.

The tumultuous experience of countless postcolonial states has shown that the idea of sovereignty has its limits. Sovereignty does not mean the right to run a malicious government and kill sections of your own people; sovereignty is a right that comes with the duty of responsible governance. Increasingly, even members of the South–South community agree: Even the African Union has a clause in its laws which allows it to intervene in one of its member states. Article 4 of the Constitutive Act of the African Union provides it the right to intervene in cases of 'war crimes, genocide and crimes against humanity'.

Sub-regional organizations in Africa have sometimes used coercive measures to avert a disaster in their midst. In 2016, the West African country of the Gambia was on the brink of a big political crisis: That year, the incumbent president Yahya Jammeh lost his bid for re-election and still refused to step down from office. He only relented after the sub-regional organization ECOWAS (or the Economic Community of West African States) threatened military action against him.

Represent Your Host's Constituency

To build relevance and influence on the international stage, New Delhi should take political positions that impact the well-being of other countries. But let me caveat this radical statement as well: This is not an appeal for reckless intervention in every country. India's foreign policy approach should be to put the political and economic stability of a nation above all else—and in pursuing this ideal, New Delhi has to be consistent in order to be credible.

In general, the stability of a country is often compromised when the population loses confidence in their government; therefore, a good rule of thumb would be to take political positions that give the popular will of the people more importance than any other competing factor. Indiscriminate violations of human rights by repressive regimes are often a precursor of trouble—which is why it makes sense, once again, for India to unequivocally voice support for the basic human rights of the people in any country.

Modern history shows that there is a considerable amount of truth to the old Gandhian philosophy: that no government can rule for too long if its own people do not consent to being governed by it. If India consistently represents the interests of the general population—even if these are often at odds with the intentions of their government—it is sure to build influence in that country *through* the general public. In practice, this means that Indian diplomats must engage with civil society organizations and political leaders from across the spectrum in countries around the world—and take appropriate action to represent their interests in the domestic and international space.

Take Syria again as an example. Syria's stability was compromised because a significant part of the Syrian population—perhaps even the majority of it—had lost all confidence in Assad's right to rule. Worse, they had no means by which to seek redressal for their exploitation by their leader. If New Delhi saw this threat to stability early, it could have pressed its diplomatic resources to do what we previously discussed (coercing Assad into yielding gradual democratic concessions; using its diplomatic presence in Syria to engage with the rebels and politically organize them; and so on). By taking these steps, India would have achieved two ends: one, a potential escape for Syria from the civil war; and two, increased credibility (and soft power) for New Delhi in the eyes of the Syrian people—which means influence over that country.

But all this is a lot easier to write about than to practise. To successfully execute this foreign policy strategy across countries, Indian diplomatic missions must consistently stay in touch with the political, economic and social realities of the country they serve in. They must be staffed with highly skilled analysts who can conduct smart and credible research and analysis of local conditions—in order to stay in touch with public opinion and represent the popular will. Indian diplomats will also need to be in constant touch with local civil society organizations at all levels. All this gets even harder to do in a country that is ruled by an authoritarian regime, which bans all political activity. In such countries, the popular will is not easily evident—and cannot be known without intelligent (and diplomatically sensitive) engagement with the people. Oftentimes, brewing discontent and a potential rebellion are difficult to sniff out, unless one is well connected with the grassroots.

People, People Everywhere

The problem for New Delhi is that all these activities take considerable human resources of high quality. And this is where India's woefully understaffed diplomatic corps is a big problem. Since most Indian missions abroad have too few diplomats at their service, almost all manpower is used up in bureaucratic work (many of which are compounded, ironically, by India's lack of influence in that country). These include issuing visas, rescuing Indian citizens in distress, and so on. The shortage of staff also means that almost all strategic thinking capacity in the Indian missions is focused exclusively on meeting India's own domestic needs through MoUs and bilateral agreements. Very little capacity is left over to focus on the *host country's* internal dynamics or *its* needs. In other words, Indian diplomats spend most of their working hours thinking about *India* rather than the country they are posted in. That is also why visits by the Indian prime minister to these countries read more like the travels of a businessman, rather than that of a global statesman: He is able to offer very little on what matters to *them*, politically.

If India had a strong intelligence-sharing partnership with the US (and other allies) across countries—like the arrangement we discussed in the last chapter—US intelligence capabilities will help make up India's own gaps. American diplomatic missions around the world already do the sort of intelligence-gathering and grassroots analysis that I am prescribing here—and a partnership in this exercise between Indian and American missions in different countries will be helpful to both India and the US.

Yet, eventually, India will need to build its own capabilities—particularly by developing and increasing its human resources deployment. The good news is that this is a problem that can be easily solved by political will in New Delhi. India's understaffed Foreign Service is not a reflection of a lack of financial or human resources in India. According to the Ministry of External Affairs, India has about 850 diplomats manning missions abroad as well as various posts at home. This is about the same size as Singapore's foreign service—a country whose economy produces only 12 per cent of the total value that India produces each year. India also has at its disposal innumerable talented young thinkers who are currently in policy schools scattered across the world. If New Delhi wanted to enrich its Foreign Service while expanding it, it could very easily tap into this rich pool of talent through lateral entry mechanisms, fellowships and other means.

The problem is that Indian politicians often think that foreign policy influence is a luxury. But instead, for India, it is now a necessity which will allow Indians to study, earn and prosper, both at home and abroad.

Change must also happen in New Delhi, not just in Indian missions overseas. There's a mismatch between India's strategic focus and its natural strengths: Much of India's strategic thinking is military-centric. Delhi foreign policy circles and think tanks are dominated by military folks—former generals and senior army officers, who specialize in India's national security problems in South Asia, and particularly the borders with Pakistan and China. This is a fallout of Indira Gandhi's militaristic, neighbourhood-centric foreign policy pivot. But the problem for New Delhi is that India's military does not have the global reach and presence to spearhead its quest for global leadership. Unlike America, India cannot—and likely never will—airdrop its troops to military bases all over the world. (And to complete the circle, since Delhi strategic thinking is very military-centric, it can't quite drive India's influence outside South Asia.)

India's global influence depends on the strength of its political and economic development; its path to global leadership is based on meeting the political and economic needs of other countries. Delhi foreign policy circles—both think tanks and the MEA—should skill themselves to reflect this fact. They should be investing heavily in analysts who study the economic and political conditions of countries all over the world, to see how India can meet their interests. By contrast, the military should serve only to defend the homeland. This is not unlike what the European Union and even China do: The EU's power derives from political and economic influence around the world—not its military. And Xi's global aspirations are based largely on political and economic efforts, such as BRI, the AIIB and party-training in Africa.

I am not, by any means, arguing that India should not develop its military presence; indeed, the military is essential in providing New Delhi the coercive strength it needs—a useful bargaining chip in assisting its political and economic efforts around the world. But military considerations should not be monopolizing the strategic blueprint for India's global aspirations. That effort should be driven by grassroots intelligence, collected across Indian diplomatic missions, and tied together by multidisciplinary and globally relevant analysis in New Delhi.

Tying the Threads Together

In conclusion of all this analysis, what should the Indian world order look like? India has strong interests in supporting the development of democracy and the furtherance of human rights around the world. India's economy will stand to gain immensely from further economic liberalization at home—and from globalization, economic openness and easier immigration policies abroad. The standardization of policymaking around the world—done by various international agencies—makes international business easier for India's burgeoning private sector.

India also has strong interests in organizing a multilateral effort towards capacity-building—to progressively develop public systems around the world. By becoming a partner in the development journeys of countries around the world, India will achieve two key goals: its own domestic transformation, and the expansion of its global relevance and influence. In matters of international security, India must become more proactive—sensing political trouble around the world before it engulfs millions of people; building alliances with countries to pursue common goals towards maintaining stability in problem areas of the world; and using this diplomatic presence to avert conflict and violence. In fragile post-conflict states, India should play a more proactive political role in nation-building.

But most importantly—to achieve all these goals—India needs to develop its own economy, refine its own state institutions, and take good care of its own multicultural democracy. India's greatest foreign policy assets lie at home: The success of the India Story is the basis of India's foreign policy influence—and its success is also important to the cause of international development. Without a fast-growing economy and the credibility of its democracy, India has no standing to become a world power.

Epilogue

The project of writing this book has been quite a journey for me: I embarked upon this initiative in early 2017 while at Columbia University, having been inspired by the ideas of the many luminaries I was fortunate to have met.

I have long been passionate about India's global power project—it is an idea whose time has come. As a globalist Indian patriot, I have forever believed that India has a compelling responsibility to the rest of the world—to use its national power for the cause of global good. This is what India's founding fathers—from Mahatma Gandhi to Bal Gangadhar Tilak, from Jawaharlal Nehru to Subhas Chandra Bose—would have wanted. Their fight and their message were always universal and global in nature: They aspired not just for their own freedom but also for the freedom of others.

This is why India's freedom struggle inspired the likes of Nelson Mandela and Martin Luther King: It was framed on the basis of universal ideals, not on notions of ethnicity. When the Indian National Congress called for *Purna Swaraj* (or complete independence) in 1929, it called for independence on the basis that fundamental human rights should be delivered to *all* the Indian

people. As I wrote in one of my essays for the Freedom Gazette—
an online portal inspired by these very ideals—the communal
Partition of India was a *secession* from these universal ideals. None
of the founding fathers of India's republic subscribed to the view
that India should be a nation based on ethnicity or narrow notions
of identity. Nehru's own globalist outlook too derived from these
universal ideals.

Yet, in recent times, I have repeatedly had to question whether
the message, objective and underlying philosophy of my book
would remain relevant. Through the second half of 2019 and the
early part of 2020 (during which time I am writing this paragraph),
the India Story has come under considerable strain. Both India's
multicultural democracy and its hallowed state institutions have
begun showing serious cracks. India's political discourse has been
poisonous for quite a while now: Politicians routinely attack
those from other communities—on religious, caste-based and
even linguistic lines. Hindu nationalism—which explicitly aspires
for an Indian national identity that is primarily for, of and by the
Hindus—is now the most dominant political ideology.

The Fragility of Institutions

As nearly everybody who is likely to read this book may know,
India introduced the religion-based Citizenship Amendment
Act (CAA) in late 2019. Plenty of commentary and analysis has
already been written on this law, including by myself, and its
Hindu nationalist undertones were not lost on the world. India
saw widespread protests from those who wished to retain its secular
founding principles. The international media mourned the death of
those universal ideals.

But what has surrounded the law has been much worse than
the law itself: India's state institutions—the backbone of India's
global power aspirations—are under great strain. In 2019, journalist

Aatish Taseer wrote a highly critical cover story for *Time* magazine on the Indian prime minister. Shortly afterwards, he found his Overseas Citizenship of India privilege cancelled on technical grounds by the Indian home ministry. In February 2020, deadly riots broke out in Delhi between those who support the CAA and those who oppose it. In the aftermath of those riots, shocking reports surfaced of the Delhi police force's demeanour during the violence: In one gruesome video circulated in the media, a group of severely injured men were beaten up and forced to sing the national anthem—right in front of police officers in riot gear. One of the men subsequently died. In March 2020, a former chief justice of the Indian Supreme Court was nominated to Parliament. The appointment triggered very valid concerns regarding the independence of the judiciary. It didn't help that the chief justice in question had presided over politically sensitive cases and had ruled in favour of the Modi government.

I cannot stress enough the importance of India's multicultural democracy, and the need for its many state institutions to remain credible. These are the elements which provide India its political stability, despite chaotic diversity. These are the elements which make economic growth possible by providing an enabling framework. And from a foreign policy point of view—these are the elements which make India relevant in international politics. The story of Indian democracy wins India goodwill in the eyes of civil society activists and citizens around the world—regardless of the political system that they live under. Credible state institutions are India's greatest strength—the *biggest asset* that India can share with the rest of the world. For India, they are the equivalent of China's infrastructural power—the developing world's envy.

Yet, alarmingly, it seems unclear if Indians as a whole are aware of the importance of their democratic set-up—or if they even acknowledge the threats that their state institutions currently face. In 2017, a Pew survey revealed the shocking result that a majority

of Indians polled—53 per cent—*support military rule*. The survey
had uncovered even worse facts: At least 55 per cent of Indians
also backed a governing system 'in which a strong leader can make
decisions without interference from parliament or the courts'. In
fact, the support for autocratic rule was higher in India than in any
other nation surveyed.[1]

Polarizing political events in India have also polarized the
diaspora abroad. As the CAA controversy raged and Kashmir was put
under curfew for months on end, Indians overseas began protesting
in front of Indian consulates and embassies across the West. In the
United States, even prominent Indian-American politicians—
including Congresswoman Pramila Jayapal, Congressman Ro
Khanna and the then Senator Kamala Harris—came out to criticize
New Delhi vocally. The cost of a fractured diaspora will prove
severe for India's foreign policy aspirations; the diaspora is by far
India's most unique weapon of influence abroad.

India's economy has also suffered in recent times. Even this
has had much to do with the state of India's state institutions. In
recent times, scholars from around the world have questioned the
credibility of India's GDP numbers, which some say are being
tampered with to make the government look good. As the Soviets
realized, without reliable data, it is impossible to make good
policy. In the pre-COVID-19 days, estimates put India's GDP
growth rate at about 3–5 per cent—a far cry from the days of the
economic juggernaut only a few years ago. With the advent of
COVID-19, India suffered the worst economic contraction of any
developing country. In October 2020, the World Bank estimated
that India's economy will shrink by almost 10 per cent in 2020–21
before possibly rebounding to a little over 5 per cent the following
fiscal year. In a country as poor as India, these numbers feel like
a prolonged recession. Millions of new graduates are entering the
workforce with nowhere to work; several are losing the jobs that
they already had.

Strangely enough, India has also begun dropping the open and liberal economic policies which created all this growth in the first place. In 2014, Prime Minister Modi campaigned for power on the basis of economic development. Many believed that, as chief minister of Gujarat, Modi had followed economic liberalization policies which made investment easier and more profitable. But as time went by, Modi began putting the Hindu nationalist political agenda ahead of the economic liberalization agenda. In recent years, India has become decidedly more protectionist and anti-global. According to the Global Trade Alert database, India had introduced the second-most number of trade restrictions among all G20 economies between 2016 and 2018 (the highest number belonged to the United States, where President Trump had been waging a trade war on multiple fronts).

All of these are worrying trends. For its global power aspirations to be realized, India should be travelling in the *opposite* direction on every one of these parameters: more economic liberalization, stronger social cohesion, and more professional and effective democratic institutions.

The Resilience of Democracy

In chapter 6, I pointed out that democracy is difficult to establish. Countries can take *decades* to cultivate a democratic culture which can sustain itself. But the corollary is also true: Once a mature democratic culture takes root, it is very difficult to be done away with. Leaders with authoritarian tendencies may come and go— but try as they might, they may never turn a mature democracy into a full-fledged tinpot dictatorship. My conviction, as I argued in chapter 2, is that India's democratic culture was one of the strongest reasons why Indira Gandhi's Emergency turned out to be a temporary blip.

What makes democracy resilient? A democratic culture means that people become well used to their rights as citizens—they speak and question freely, protest at will, and petition various influencers for change, even if such actions are met with sanctions. In India, despite reports of intimidation, the press continues to write and comment freely on all political and public affairs, with the exception of the television media. But even on television, there have been some standouts: In 2019, Ravish Kumar and Nidhi Razdan—both of the NDTV news group—won the Ramon Magsaysay Award and the International Press Institute Award respectively for their efforts to hold the government accountable.

State institutions are resilient too. Corruption and centralization can impact the independence of institutions even in a democracy, but if a leader silences ninety-nine institutions, he will invariably find the 100th institution pushing back. In the aftermath of the Delhi riots, Justice S. Muralidhar in the Delhi High Court pulled up the Delhi Police for its actions (or inactions) during the violence. In scathing remarks, he also tore into leaders from the ruling party for their hateful speeches in the run-up to the violence. Shortly afterwards, as he was being transferred to the Punjab and Haryana High Court, he received a raucous send-off from a huge gathering of judges and lawyers, who lauded his conscientious discharge of duty.

Since well-established fundamental rights and freedoms are difficult to remove overnight in a country where democracy has taken root, Indians continue to discuss and push back against excesses from their government. Protests continued across India against the proposed citizenship tests for months, before disbanding due to COVID-19. Social media has helped raise awareness, in recent times, especially among younger voters who continue to seek to uphold the liberal values of their freedom struggle.

But no democracy—whether India or the United States—should take its institutions and rights for granted. The resilience of democracy is not due to divine intervention; it is due to the persistent efforts of the citizens themselves to continue their democratic traditions. In India, the democratic culture seems to be well and truly deep-rooted. But Indians must keep it that way.

The Legacy of Openness

Unlike China, India has never managed to homogenize itself. It almost appears that India's destiny is that of a multicultural civilization. In the last 5000 years, mighty emperors have come and gone in the futile effort to homogenize India. They all tried to use the force of the state and its mighty propaganda apparatus to goad Indians—as a whole—to follow a certain defined monoculture. And they all failed—from Ashoka who propagated Buddhism, to Aurangzeb who propagated Islam, and even the British missionaries who propagated Christianity. Ashoka's efforts to convert an entire nation to Buddhism were, in fact, more successful in Sri Lanka than in India.

Regardless of their individual cultural backgrounds, Indians are inherently global in nature—and they have always been. India has long been the land where that which is foreign comes to become Indian. This cultural openness—practised over several generations—is singularly responsible for the dizzying diversity which defines India today. A short drive through Delhi, the epicentre of the 2020 communal riots, is sufficient to establish this point. From one neighbourhood to another, visitors to India's capital city can see a stunning diversity of architecture—from ancient Hindu temples to Islamic/Mughal monuments and the Victorian buildings where India's government presently resides.

This inherent openness towards the world is the most intrinsic and natural element which is likely to sustain—and even strengthen—India's multicultural democracy against any efforts to homogenize the country. If mighty emperors through the ages could not shut the doors and homogenize India, despite all their resources and authoritarianism, it is impossible that any political dispensation could do it in the republic, against the force of a well-rooted democratic culture.

But this means that Indians must—as a people—retain their globalist character. In recent generations, Indians have become increasingly insular, even as they have become culturally globalized. In the Pew survey I just quoted, many Indians supported military rule and authoritarianism. Part of this is due to ignorance: Few Indians know much about the rest of the world and are therefore unaware of the stories of Indonesia under Sukarno, Chile under Pinochet, or Uganda under Idi Amin—all of whom were military rulers. Fewer still know about how authoritarianism and centralization of power have led countries into the vicious cycle of violence and civil war around the world. As a result, Indians have become *tired* of their peaceful democracy, seeing in it only corruption, inefficiency and policy paralysis.

A large part of the blame here must necessarily be apportioned to the media. Indian media outlets—as a rule—provide very limited coverage of the world. A disproportionate amount of airtime is given to entirely pointless and paranoid discussions on just Pakistan and, more recently, China. Most Indian journalists themselves have rarely, if ever, spent any reasonable amount of time working overseas or observing international affairs.

I argued in the preface that limited coverage of international affairs is in large part responsible for India's insular foreign policy. But a more proactive and internationalist foreign policy may by itself bring about a change in this matter. If New Delhi took an active interest in issues of global concern in faraway lands, acted proactively in the manner in which we have discussed previously, and built up India's relevance around the world, the Indian media will have to inevitably expand itself. American media outlets have stronger international coverage and presence, in part because of Washington's own foreign policy actions around the world. In this manner, a proactive and outward-looking foreign policy may even get rid of India's insularity—and have remarkable positive effects for its own multiculturalism and democratic traditions.

In writing this book, I am hopeful of a transformation for India, its foreign policy and the rest of the world. But I am also very conscious of the fact that most of what I propose will not— or, perhaps, should not—happen immediately or all at once. My objective is to spark public debate and discussion on the issues which I have addressed. In due time, I am hopeful that the changes that Indians undertake together will result in a more open, globalist and proactive India—one which will usher in an era of Indian power for the cause of global good.

Acknowledgements

I have always been an avid traveller and globetrotter, thanks in large part to my perennially peripatetic family. I first boarded a flight when I was about a year old. Since then, I have marvelled at how much one can learn simply by flying around the world. My love for travelling engendered my curiosity for the world's many nations and dizzying diversity—which in turn inspired my love of writing about the world.

Yet, despite years of writing in various capacities on myriad subjects, I had hardly hoped that I would ever be able to write an entire book. My journeys around the world made this book possible, but in many ways, writing this book was itself a journey. It took me back in time through my own memories, brought me into contact with some very interesting people in various walks of life in several different countries, and challenged many of my previously deep-seated convictions about the world.

As I began conceiving and compiling this book, my base camp was set up at Columbia University. Indeed, this book would not have been possible without Columbia and its extraordinary resources; it is a true-blood Columbia product. I will forever cherish the two years that I spent at the School of International and Public Affairs (or SIPA, as we 'Seeple' call it) as some of the best years of my life, and I hope that I will soon find myself back there in some capacity.

I am particularly indebted to the many brilliant scholars and professors who gave me their time and indulged me in many a fascinating conversation, sometimes running on for hours: Elisabeth Lindenmayer, whose many years at the UN helped shape my thinking on issues of international security and diplomacy; Richard Gowan, whose ability to conjure witty and sharp takes on international affairs I will always envy; Ambassador Kishore Mahbubani, whose provocative and contrarian views on many international issues always pushed me to think outside the box.

There were countless others as well who made various contributions to my work and I should acknowledge every single colleague whom I was lucky to meet at Columbia. Each of them came from a different corner of the world and brought stories that informed this book. I was lucky to have had passionate debates on our life and times with friends, colleagues and neighbours who hailed from everywhere—from Mexico to Morocco. Some of them were pillars of emotional support to me during some very difficult moments; it would be criminal of me not to acknowledge my best friends Aparna Singh and Astha Arya here, along with several others who played important roles in my life at Columbia.

I must recount some particularly amusing episodes which showed the dedication to academic pursuit among the Columbia family. Elisabeth Lindenmayer once missed a meeting at Columbia because she was so absorbed in debating with me about the United Nations and relating to me her encounters with Kofi Annan, Helmut Kohl and Angela Merkel. Ambassador Mahbubani, who represented Singapore at the UN, and Ambassador John Hirsch, the former US envoy to Sierra Leone, provided especially invaluable inputs during the early stages of my work, along with fascinating first-hand accounts from the world of diplomacy. I often regretted that I did not bring them both into the same room; their opposing takes on many issues would have made for a fascinating debate, but I was a grateful beneficiary of their time, and the fact that they disagreed with each other on some issues only helped broaden my own horizons. Vishakha Desai and Robert Oxnam were both invaluable resources for the chapter on China, as was my friend and colleague Mia Li—formerly of the *New York Times*—who is a walking encyclopaedia on her home country and always has the most inimitable manner of explaining it.

My eventful time with the Indian delegation to the UN in New York gave me several fascinating stories that will someday make it into my memoirs. Owing to my professional and academic commitments at Columbia, I was only able to give my full time and attention to them for a couple of months. Yet, the countless anecdotes and provocative thoughts that I received through my inspirational colleagues there have been invaluable additions to this book. I will be forever grateful to Ambassador Syed Akbaruddin for the mentorship that he provided me and the encouragement he gave me during my time with him. It was my highest honour to play a small part, along with his incredible team, in helping India win a historic election to the International Court of Justice in 2017. India was elected over the United Kingdom in an extraordinary sequence of events that taught me countless lessons about diplomacy at the UN.

Years ago, I took to writing on international affairs because of Fareed Zakaria, whose work has inspired many a young writer like myself. But I was especially fortunate to have met him in his CNN office in New York during the early conceptual stages of this book. True to his name as an extraordinary writer, Fareed helped shape the early layout and outline of this book, enriching it with his fascinating thoughts and encouraging my own radical thinking on Indian foreign policy. Towards the end of that discussion, he said, 'It's about time someone wrote about these things.' Every time I found myself wanting and my energy sapped, I went back to those words.

Further inspiration came from Shashi Tharoor, another man who needs no introduction to the world. I have always been touched by the amount of time that Dr Tharoor spends in identifying and encouraging young writers and thinkers, despite his eternally packed schedule and many commitments. I have personally been among those lucky beneficiaries. Dr Tharoor found my early raw work as a blogger while I was still at the tender age of seventeen, and he has been a source of motivation ever since. I could not have made the several bold and important professional choices I have made in life without his encouragement—and this book would not have become a reality without those decisions.

I will be remiss if I did not also acknowledge the help and support of my idealistic and passionate colleagues at Freedom Gazette, who are helping me build a ground-breaking initiative for a better India. My fellow co-founders, Ashima Kohli and Anuj Raghuram, were a part of my research efforts and helped conceive the idea of the Freedom Gazette over the course of those efforts. The Gazette is now my long-term passionate project for life— alongside whatever else I might be doing. I am heartened that it has already attracted interest from many—both my fellow young Indians and foreigners who hope that India will fulfil her golden destiny. I will be privileged to work alongside them in the years to come for the progress and evolution of Indian politics, society and policy.

Among those whom I came into contact with through the work of Freedom Gazette was Shairee Malhotra—a fellow writer and academic who now serves as the Gazette's foreign affairs editor. I will be forever indebted to Shairee for the many selfless hours that she spent in editing my raw manuscript. Her wisdom and balanced thinking provided the perfect foil for my radical ideas, many of which she helped polish through her ingeniousness and intellectual rigour. In her, I have found a great friend for life to share many of my professional passions with.

Finally, no words are sufficient to appreciate the sacrifices of my family—my father, mother, sister and grandfather. Despite tremendous anxiety, they have often supported my unconventional career choices, including the socially difficult decision to meander out of a life in mechanical engineering (in which, like many Indians, I had done my undergraduate studies). I have been lucky to be among them, trying to imbibe a few of their qualities to help me with my work—my mother's innate talent with words; my father's scientific inquisitiveness; my grandfather's penchant for always questioning the status quo; and my sister's freewheeling creativity.

Growing up, my late grandmother was a pillar of support and a source of unconditional belief in my abilities. I often wish that I could believe in myself as confidently as she had. Despite having struggled to find formal education, my grandmother had an unquenchable thirst for knowledge of all kinds and a remarkable common sense in place of unthinking blind belief. This book is wholeheartedly dedicated to her and her inspiration.

There are several others whom I must name in these pages, including Prof. Brijesh Nair of VIT University, who played an unparalleled role in my development as a young man, and countless friends and colleagues who indulge me in absorbing discussions almost every day. Many of these discussions have been reflected in this book and across my many essays in the international media.

I must also greatly appreciate the folks at Penguin—especially my editors, Radhika Marwah and Shreya Chakravertty, who believed right away that this book deserves to be read and have worked tirelessly ever since to develop and polish it into this final product. Upon reading the manuscript, Radhika had said that she sees many books in me. Here's hoping that this is only the first among them!

Notes

Preface

1. Kat Devlin, 'A Sampling of Public Opinion in India', Pew Research Center, 2019, https://www.pewresearch.org/global/2019/03/25/a-sampling-of-public-opinion-in-india.

Introduction

1. Richmond Barbour, Power and Distant Display: Early English "Ambassadors" in Moghul India (Huntington Library Quarterly, University of Pennsylvania Press, 1998,).
2. Matthew Hayden, *Standing My Ground* (HarperCollins, 2010).
3. Srinath Raghavan, 'When Indian Troops Entered Congo 55 Years Ago', *Livemint*, 19 September 2016, http://www.livemint.com/Opinion/9D5XT497AEYYluFn3moa2H/When-Indian-troops-entered-Congo-55-years-ago.html.
4. Bruce Riedel, *JFK's Forgotten Crisis: Tibet, the CIA, and Sino-Indian War* (The Brookings Institution, 2015).

Chapter 1: The Great Indian Rope Walk

1. Patrick Olivelle, *King, Governance, and Law in Ancient India: Kautilya's Arthashastra, A New Annotated Translation* (Oxford: Oxford University Press, 2013).
2. Stephen Cohen, *India: Emerging Power* (Brookings Institution Press, 2002).
3. Barbara D. Metcalf and Thomas R. Metcalf, *A Concise History of India* (Cambridge: Cambridge University Press, 2002).
4. Cohen, *India: Emerging Power*.
5. Manmohan Singh, 'PM's speech at the Council on Foreign Relations', New York, 24 September 2004, https://archivepmo. nic.in/drmanmohansingh/speech-details.php?nodeid=20.
6. Prime Minister's Office, 'PM to Heads of Indian Missions', Press Information Bureau, Government of India, 2015, http://pib.nic. in/newsite/PrintRelease.aspx?relid=115241.

Chapter 2: The India Story

1. BizCommunity, 'The 10 Greatest South Africans of All Time', 27 September 2004, https://www.bizcommunity.com/ Article/196/423/4673.html.
2. Ramachandra Guha, *India After Gandhi* (Picador India, 2012).
3. Shashi Tharoor, 'Nehru and Democracy', *Asian Age*, 18 November 2018, http://www.asianage.com/360-degree/181118/nehru-and-democracy.html.
4. Denny Indrayana, *Indonesian Constitutional Reform 1999–2002*, https:// www.kas.de/c/document_library/get_file?uuid=d0f69252-c918-5c5c-770a-8193befdf986&groupId=252038.
5. Ide Anak Agung Gde Agung, *Twenty Years Indonesian Foreign Policy 1945–1965* (Mouton & Co, 1973).
6. Guha, *India After Gandhi*.
7. Ibid.
8. Kuldip Nayar, 'Remembering Indira Gandhi on Her 35th Death Anniversary', *Telegraph*, 31 October 2019, https://www.

telegraphindia.com/culture/remembering-indira-gandhi-on-her-35th-death-anniversary/cid/1715657.

9. Jim Sleeper, 'Lee Kuan Yew's Hard Truths', OpenDemocracy, 2015, https://www.opendemocracy.net/en/lee-kuan-yews-hard-truths.

10. William Borders, 'The Economy and Emergency in India', *New York Times*, 23 January 1977, https://www.nytimes.com/1977/01/23/archives/the-economy-and-emergency-in-india.html.

11. R. Nagaraj, 'Growth Rate of India's GDP, 1950–51 to 1987–88', 30 June 1990, *Economic and Political Weekly*, Vol. 2, http://www.igidr.ac.in/nag/Growth%20Rate%20of%20India's%20GDP.pdf.

12. Fareed Zakaria, *The Post-American World* (Penguin, 2008).

13. *The Economist*, 'Asia's Trade Negotiators Decide They Can No Longer Wait for India', 7 November 2019, https://www.economist.com/asia/2019/11/07/asias-trade-negotiators-decide-they-can-no-longer-wait-for-india.

14. Saritha Rai, 'India's New "English Only" Generation', *New York Times*, 1 June 2012.

15. Zubair Ahmed, 'Bollywood's Expanding Reach', BBC, 2012.

16. George Gao, 'Why Is China So . . . Uncool?' 8 March 2017, Foreign Policy.

17. The Observatory of Economic Complexity, Country Profiles, 12 November 2020, https://oec.world/en/profile/country/ind/.

18. Weizhen Tan, 'Chinese Corporate Debt Is the "Biggest Threat" to the Global Economy, Says Moody's Chief Economist', *CNBC*, 17 December 2019, https://www.cnbc.com/2019/12/17/chinas-corporate-debt-is-biggest-threat-to-global-economy-moodys.html.

19. United Nations Department of Economic and Social Affairs (Population Division), World Population Prospects 2019, United Nations, 22 March 2020, https://population.un.org/wpp/DataQuery/.

20. *Economic Times,* '50% India's Working-Age Population Out of Labour Force, Says Report', 4 February 2019,

https://economictimes.indiatimes.com/jobs/50-indias-working-age-population-out-of-labour-force-says-report/articleshow/67830482.cms?from=mdr.

Chapter 3: The Tinderbox

1. Kathleen D. Morrison, 'Commerce and Culture in South Asia: Perspectives from Archaeology and History', *Annual Review of Anthropology*, Vol. 26 (1997): 87–108.
2. Kristi L. Wiley, *Historical Dictionary of Jainism* (2004).
3. Rachel Havrelock, 'Pipelines in the Sand: The Middle East After Sykes–Picot', 17 May 2016, *Foreign Affairs*, https://www.foreignaffairs.com/articles/middle-east/2016-05-17/pipelines-sand.
4. Akhilesh Pillalamarri and Aswin Subanthore, 'What Do the Bhutanese People Think About Doklam?' 14 August 2017, Diplomat, https://thediplomat.com/2017/08/what-do-the-bhutanese-people-think-about-doklam.
5. Constantino Xavier, 'The Quest for Regional Connectivity', *Hindustan Times*, 5 February 2020, https://www.hindustantimes.com/analysis/the-quest-for-regional-connectivity-opinion/story-DZU7JLrCXBebOmZHkwUbBL.html.
6. Associated Press, 'Pakistani Police Demolish Mosque of Minority Ahmadi Sect', *VOA News*, 28 October 2019, https://www.voanews.com/south-central-asia/pakistani-police-demolish-mosque-minority-ahmadi-sect.
7. *Asian Age*, 'Sheikh Hasina: Why Is CAA Necessary?' 20 January 2020, https://www.asianage.com/india/all-india/200120/sheikh-hasina-why-is-caa-necessary.html.
8. Suhasini Haidar, 'All Afghans Have Been Persecuted, Says Hamid Karzai', *The Hindu*, 19 January 2020, https://www.thehindu.com/news/national/all-afghans-have-been-persecuted-karzai/article30600574.ece.
9. Xavier, 'The Quest for Regional Connectivity'.

Chapter 4: The Chinese Dream

1. Henry Kissinger, *On China* (Penguin Press, 2011).
2. Valerie Hansen, *The Silk Road: A New History* (Oxford University Press, 2012).
3. John Major, *Silk Road: Spreading Ideas and Innovations* (Asia Society).
4. Amartya Sen, *The Argumentative Indian* (Farrar, Strauss and Giroux, 2005).
5. Orville Schell and John Delury, *Wealth and Power: China's Long March to the 21st Century* (2013).
6. *China Daily*, 'Background: Connotations of Chinese Dream', 5 March 2014, http://www.chinadaily.com.cn/china/2014npcandcppcc/2014-03/05/content_17324203.htm.
7. Steven Stashwick, 'China's South China Sea Militarization Has Peaked', Foreign Policy, 19 August 2019,. https://foreignpolicy.com/2019/08/19/chinas-south-china-sea-militarization-has-peaked/.
8. Gabriel Wildau, 'China's Reliance on Infrastructure Stimulus At Record High', *Financial Times*, 24 August 2017, https://www.ft.com/content/1fe4e1e8-88b0-11e7-bf50-e1c239b45787.
9. Gwynn Guilford, 'China's Debt Disease Might Wreck Its Uncrashable Housing Market', 11 June 2019, Quartz, https://qz.com/1615596/chinas-debt-disease-is-infecting-its-housing-market/.
10. Morgan Stanley Research, 'Inside China's Plan to Create a Modern Silk Road', 2018, https://www.morganstanley.com/ideas/china-belt-and-road.
11. Ernst and Young, 'EY Africa Attractiveness Report 2019', 2019.
12. Mogopodi Lekorwe, et al., 'China's Growing Presence in Africa Wins Largely Positive Popular Reviews', Afrobarometer, 2016.
13. Porter Morgan and Jason Nicholson, 'Does China Have a Looming Africa Problem?' *Diplomat*, 19 September 2016.
14. David Dollar, 'United States–China Two-Way Direct Investment: Opportunities and Challenges', Brookings Institution, 2015.

15. Elizabeth Whitman, 'Omar Al-Bashir China Visit 2015: Despite ICC Warrant, Sudanese President Returns Amid Turmoil Over Economic, Military Ties', *International Business Times*, 31 August 2015.

16. James Peck, *Washington's China: The National Security World, the Cold War, and the Origins of Globalism* (University of Massachusetts Press, 2006), pp. 46–47.

17. United States Office of Soviet Analysis, 'A Comparison of the US and Soviet Economies: Evaluating the Performance of the Soviet System', United States Directorate of Intelligence, 1985, https://www.cia.gov/library/readingroom/docs/DOC_0000497165.pdf.

18. Lily Kuo, 'China's Model of Economic Development Is Becoming More Popular in Africa than America's', Quartz, 28 October 2016, https://qz.com/africa/820841/chinas-model-of-economic-development-is-becoming-more-popular-in-africa-than-americas/.

19. Yun Sun, 'Political Party Training: China's Ideological Push in Africa?' Brookings Institution, 2016, https://www.brookings.edu/blog/africa-in-focus/2016/07/05/political-party-training-chinas-ideological-push-in-africa/.

20. James Kraska, 'China Is Legally Responsible for COVID-19 Damage and Claims Could Be in the Trillions', War on the Rocks, 23 March 2020, https://warontherocks.com/2020/03/china-is-legally-responsible-for-covid-19-damage-and-claims-could-be-in-the-trillions/.

21. *China Daily*, 'Background: Connotations of Chinese Dream'.

22. Kuang Keng, 'The 12 Strangest Words Censored In China (And Why They Are Banned From Weibo)', *International Business Times*, 6 March 2015, https://www.ibtimes.com/pulse/12-strangest-words-censored-china-why-they-are-banned-weibo-1951154.

23. Human Rights Watch, *China: End Denial About Tiananmen Massacre* (New York: Human Rights Watch, 2015).

24. Li Xin, 'India Through Chinese Eyes', *World Policy Journal* (Winter 2013).

25. Anirban Bhaumik, 'Chinese Dissidents to Meet in India to Seek Democracy', *Deccan Herald*, 21 April 2016.

Chapter 5: The Old Guard

1. Ramachandra Guha, *India After Gandhi* (Picador India, 2012).
2. Samuel Eliot Morison, 'The Origin of the Monroe Doctrine, 1775–1823', *Economica* (February 1924): https://www.jstor.org/stable/2547870?seq=1.
3. Woodrow Wilson, 'War Message to Congress', United States Congress, https://wwi.lib.byu.edu/index.php/Wilson%27s_War_Message_to_Congress.
4. Ibid.
5. John B. Judis, *The Chosen Nation: The Influence of Religion on U.S. Foreign Policy* (Carnegie Endowment for International Peace, 2005), https://carnegieendowment.org/files/PB37.judis.FINAL.pdf.
6. Guha, *India After Gandhi*.
7. G. John Ikenberry, 'Getting Hegemony Right', *National Interest* (Spring 2001): 17–24.
8. Ramachandra, *India After Gandhi*.
9. Department of Economic Affairs, Government of India, 'Fact Sheet on Overseas Direct Investment', https://www.ibef.org/economy/indian-investments-abroad, https://dea.gov.in/overseas-direct-investment?page=1.
10. Asian Infrastructure Investment Bank, 'Articles of Agreement', https://www.aiib.org/en/about-aiib/basic-documents/_download/articles-of-agreement/basic_document_english-bank_articles_of_agreement.pdf.
11. World Bank, 'Annual Report 2019: Lending Data', 2019, http://pubdocs.worldbank.org/en/724041569960954210/WBAR19-Lending-Data.pdf.

Chapter 6: The New Guard

1. Consultancy Middle East, 'GCC Consulting Market Breaks $3 Billion Barrier with 9% Growth', 2019, https://www.consultancy-me.com/news/2216/gcc-consulting-market-breaks-3-billion-barrier-with-9-growth.

2. IANS, 'India's Poll Panel Has Sent Electoral Observers to 10 Countries', FirstPost, 7 July 2013.

3. Tom Burgis, *The Looting Machine: Warlords, Oligarchs, Corporations, Smugglers, and the Theft of Africa's Wealth* (PublicAffairs, 2015).

4. Joe Myers, '19 of the World's 20 Youngest Countries Are in Africa', World Economic Forum, 2019, https://www.weforum. org/agenda/2019/08/youngest-populations-africa.

5. Issandr El Amrani, 'How Much of Libya Does the Islamic State Control?' International Crisis Group, 2016, https://www. crisisgroup.org/middle-east-north-africa/north-africa/libya/ how-much-libya-does-islamic-state-control.

6. BBC World News, 'Iraq War in Figures', 2011, https://www. bbc.com/news/world-middle-east-11107739.

7. Rafid Jaboori, 'Iraqi Sunnis' Long Struggle Since Saddam', BBC, https://www.bbc.com/news/world-middle-east-25559872.

8. Munqith al-Dagher, 'How Iraqi Sunnis Really Feel about the Islamic State', *Washington Post*, 24 March 2015, https://www.washingtonpost.com/news/monkey-cage/ wp/2015/03/24/how-iraqi-sunnis-really-feel-about-the-islamic-state/?arc404=true.

9. António Guterres, 'Meeting the Prevention Challenge', *UN Chronicle*, United Nations, 2017, https://www.un.org/en/ chronicle/article/meeting-prevention-challenge.

10. P.S. Raghavan, 'Talk by Shri PS Raghavan, SS (DP) on Development Partnership Administration (DPA)', Manohar Parrikar Institute for Defence Studies and Analyses, 2013, https:// idsa.in/event/TalkbyShriPSRaghavan.

Epilogue

1. Richard Wike, et al., 'Democracy Widely Supported, Little Backing for Rule by Strong Leader or Military', Pew Research Center, 2017, https://www.pewresearch.org/global/2017/10/16/ democracy-widely-supported-little-backing-for-rule-by-strong-leader-or-military.